T0208991

# A Troublesome Man

## About the Life of Dr. Ptolemy Reid, Prime Minister of Guyana 1980–1984

*Stella Bagot*

**BALBOA.**
PRESS
A DIVISION OF HAY HOUSE

Balboa Press books may be ordered through booksellers or by contacting:

Balboa Press
A Division of Hay House
1663 Liberty Drive
Bloomington, IN 47403
www.balboapress.com
1 (877) 407-4847

Because of the dynamic nature of the Internet, any web addresses or links contained in this book may have changed since publication and may no longer be valid. The views expressed in this work are solely those of the author and do not necessarily reflect the views of the publisher, and the publisher hereby disclaims any responsibility for them.

The author of this book does not dispense medical advice or prescribe the use of any technique as a form of treatment for physical, emotional, or medical problems without the advice of a physician, either directly or indirectly. The intent of the author is only to offer information of a general nature to help you in your quest for emotional and spiritual well-being. In the event you use any of the information in this book for yourself, which is your constitutional right, the author and the publisher assume no responsibility for your actions.

This book is a work of non-fiction. Unless otherwise noted, the author and the publisher make no explicit guarantees as to the accuracy of the information contained in this book and in some cases, names of people and places have been altered to protect their privacy.

Any people depicted in stock imagery provided by Getty Images are models, and such images are being used for illustrative purposes only.
Certain stock imagery © Getty Images.

Print information available on the last page.

ISBN: 978-1-9822-0684-0 (sc)
ISBN: 978-1-9822-0682-6 (hc)
ISBN: 978-1-9822-0683-3 (e)

Library of Congress Control Number: 2018907199

Balboa Press rev. date: 06/22/2018

I dedicate this book to the memory of my beloved mother, Ada Bagot, and to my aunt and uncle, Serene and Oscar Adams with whom I lived as a child.

# CONTENTS

# ACKNOWLEDGEMENTS

I owe a ton of gratitude to Kelly Gannon whose assistance with the typing of a considerable part of my manuscript was the stimulus I needed to get ahead with the work at hand. Trisha Karasik helped in providing insightful criticism of the opening chapters. Yvonne Harewood shared her knowledge of the subject of this book. Encouragement from members of my biological family and the interest of my church family propelled me on. Of course, I owe a great deal of gratitude to long-standing friends, teachers and colleagues without whose support I would not have had the ability and confidence to pursue this project. This biography would not have materialized without the humble agreement and collaboration of Dr. Reid himself. He sat down with me for long hours to recount the experiences of his early life, gave me access to his family, employees and friends, and invited me to accompany him to the many celebrations in his honour. Using the resources of the Georgetown Public Library, I was able to glean some information on Dr. Reid's political career.

# A Brief History of the Political Background of Modern Day Guyana

Guyana, formerly British Guiana, is a small country, approximately 83,000 square miles (the size of England and Scotland) on the northern coast of South America. It is adjacent to Venezuela to the west, Suriname (formerly Dutch Guiana) to the east and Brazil to the south and west. The country was, in the course of its modern history, governed by colonial powers changing hands between the Dutch, French, Spanish, and, most recently for about a century and a half, the British.

It is believed that British Guiana was discovered by Spanish sailors in 1499, and during the 16th and early 17th century, explorations for the city of El Dorado took place in the region. The earliest known settlement was established in the Pomeroon by the Dutch in 1581, but it was destroyed by Spaniards and Indians in 1596. A new fort was established at Kykoveral on the Essequibo, one of the three main rivers: Essequibo, Demerara and Berbice, which flow in a northerly direction to the Atlantic Ocean. "The colony was subsequently controlled by the Dutch West India Company. The Dutch held the territory though yielding sometimes to the English, French and Portuguese -until 1796, when it was captured by a British fleet. It was restored to the Dutch in 1802, but was retaken in 1803" by the British. (*Guyana Yearbook 1964,* 7 – 9). In 1814, Britain paid three million pounds for the colony in the peace settlement after the Napoleonic wars, and in 1831 the land formally became British Guiana (Nascimento and Burrowes, xiv)

When the Dutch surrendered to the British in 1803, the 'articles of Capitulation' stipulated that the British accept that 'the laws and usages of the colony shall remain in force and be respected.' Chief among those laws and usages was the system of government. A 'Combined Court' made up of officials appointed by the colonial power and an elected majority of financial representatives drawn from the body of sugar planters, administered the territory. The British perpetuated this system of colonial administration (Nascimento and Burrowes, xv).

The original inhabitants of British Guiana were Amerindians. Most of them [later] lived in the interior forests and savannahs of the country. In the seventeenth and eighteen centuries, slaves were imported from Africa to work on sugar and cotton plantations. After the abolition of slavery in 1834 planters, in order to meet the scarcity and rising cost of labour, began to import workers from India, China and Madeira. Many of the Portuguese from Madeira turned to trade, and soon amassed considerable fortunes. Some of the Chinese and Indians who were brought under the indenture system returned to their homes at the end of the period of their indenture, but most of them remained as farmers and traders, becoming citizens of British Guiana. (*Guyana Year Book 1964,* 7).

> Most of the people of Guyana live on the coastal plains. "Many of the Afro- Guyanese former slaves [had] moved to the towns and became the majority urban population, whereas the Indo-Guyanese remained predominantly rural" (*Countries of the World and Their Leaders Yearbook 2013,* 981).
>
> In the 1930s, workers and their representatives reacted in opposition to colonialism. Moreover, organizations such as the Civil Service Association(CSA) and the League of Colored Peoples (L.C.P.) had voiced their protest

against discriminatory practices particularly in the 1940s. There were constitutional advances in 1943 and 1945, and during the latter part of the 1940s, Cheddi Jagan, a Guianese dentist of East Indian descent, had almost single-handedly waged war against colonialism and its allies (Lutchman, 219).

"The PPP [People's Progressive Party led by Dr. Cheddi Jagan] was organized as a mass party in 1950, by which time a certain measure of constitutional advance, including the grant of universal adult suffrage, was well within reach" (Lutchman, 221). Jagan was joined by Forbes Burnham who had just returned from England after qualifying as a lawyer with high honours (*Guyana Hand Book 1974,* 13). "A new and advanced constitution [of 1953] . . . provided for universal adult suffrage, a bicameral legislature and a ministerial system" (*Guyana Year Book 1964,* 9). Together the two young Guianese won 18 of the 24 seats of the elections held under adult suffrage for the first time in 1953. "The constitution, then the most advanced in the Caribbean was suspended after the party had been in power for 133 days. An interim government was installed and it lasted for four years" (*Guyana Hand Book 1974,* 13). From October 1953, when "this advanced constitution was suspended . . . until August 1957, when a return was made to partly elected government, the legislature and the Executive Council had no elected members, but consisted of official and nominated members only" (*Guyana Year Book 1964,* 9).

Probably the PPP won its overwhelming victory at the polls in 1953 due to its multi-racial make-up. "The appeal of the PPP to East Indians and Negroes was due mainly to the personalities of Cheddi Jagan [an East Indian] and Forbes Burnham [a Negro] ... [but] there were serious ideological differences within the ranks of the party (Cmd 9274 *Report of the British Guiana . . . 1954,* 31ff)" (Lutchman, 222).

There was a split in the ranks of the PPP in 1955, with the Jaganite and Burnhamite factions each claiming to be the only authentic PPP. "Although racial considerations were by no means originally involved in the split, by the start of the campaign in connection with the 1957 general elections there were charges and counter-charges of parties appealing to certain racial groups" (Lutchman, 224). "Apan jaat, a call to vote for one's race" became a popular phrase bandied about at the time (www.landof sixpeoples.com/news02gyltns203205.htm).

The 1957 election resulted in a landslide victory for the Jaganite faction of the PPP, and shortly after the election, the Burnhamite faction changed its name to the People's National Congress (PNC) (Lutchman, 225).

Apart from demonstrating an increased polarisation along racial lines, the 1957 general election also revealed how difficult it was for the PNC to win power at any subsequent elections under the first-past-the-post system. . . It was evident that the PPP was at a decided advantage over the PNC as its supporters resided mainly in the rural areas where the majority of constituencies were located . . . It was . . . predictable that the P.N.C. would have agitated for a change in the electoral system (Lutchman, 225-226).

"At the 1960 constitutional conference it was agreed to have a two-chambered legislature. In August, 1961, elections were held under a new constitution which gave the territory full internal self-government" (*Guyana Year Book 1964*, 9). "[E]lections were held under First Past the Post and the PPP gained 22 seats of the 35 member House" (*Guyana Handbook 1974*, 13).

"The years following the 1961 general elections were some of the most eventful in the history of Guyana . . . the two major political parties grew further apart and their disagreement frequently took a violent form" (Lutchman, 226). . . . "The first in the series of crises occurred in

1962" when the government presented its "budget to the legislature in February of that year". The Kaldor budget (as it was referred to) "encountered very strong opposition from the PNC and the UF [the United Force was a conservative party launched in October 1960), some of the business interests, newspapers and the trade union movement . . . the evidence suggests that opposition was advanced with a view to gaining political advantage, not so much from principle". In any case, the consequences of the confrontation between the government and its opponents "were serious for the country . . . [there was] rioting, and arson, looting and violence, causing the death of five men, injury to eight, and destruction of property estimated at around $11 million in the business centre of the [capital] city of Georgetown. Race relations were severely strained" (Lutchman, 228).

"The principle of independence for the country having been accepted, an independence conference was held in October 1962" (*Guyana Year Book 1964*, 9), but considering the preceding turmoil,

It was . . . of little surprise when the leaders of the three parties failed to reach agreement on a number of points of the Constitutional Conference held in London . . . The following year, 1963, witnessed further disturbances. On this occasion the centre of controversy was a proposed labour relations bill which sought to give the government the power to decide the recognition of unions for purposes of representation of workers . . . The result of this proposed legislation, which eventually lapsed, was the longest general strike in the British Commonwealth with consequent serious economic damage to the country's fortunes. The strike, which lasted 80 days, was again the occasion of racial violence and bitterness (Lutchman, 228-229).

So, when once again the leaders re-convened for a constitutional conference in October 1963, they failed to come to an agreement (Lutchman, 229; *Guyana Year Book 1964*, 9).

The three leaders representing the government and the opposition – Dr. Jagan (PPP), Mr. Burnham (PNC), Mr. D'Aguiar (UF) – "informed the British Colonial Secretary, Mr. Duncan Sandys, in a Joint letter," that they couldn't reach an agreement and

requested him to impose a solution with which they could abide. A few days later Mr. Sandys announced that there would be no independence at present; instead there would be fresh elections during 1964 under the system of Proportional Representation, with the voting age of 21 years. After these elections, a conference would be called in London to settle any remaining constitutional issues and to fix a date for independence (*Guyana Year Book*, 1964, 9).

On December 7, 1964, the people of then British Guiana went to the polls to elect 53 members of the new legislature. Seven political parties contested the elections held for the first time under the system of proportional representation. The results for the three major parties were People Progressive Party 24 seats with 45.84 per cent of votes; People's National Congress 22 seats with 40.52 per cent and United Force 7 seats with 12.41 per cent of votes (*Guyana Year Book 1965*, 8).

"Although the PPP emerged as the single party with the most seats, Dr. Jagan was not able to form a government under the system of proportional representation. Mr. Burnham was therefore invited by the governor to do so, after the United Force had expressed its willingness to support the PNC. A PNC/UF coalition government consequently emerged with Mr. Burnham as Premier and Mr. D'Aguiar as finance minister." (*Guyana Year Book 1965*, 9).

The *Guyana Year Book 1966* announces that "On May 26, 1966, the new nation of Guyana will emerge sovereign and independent. Under the new constitution Guyana will have a monarchical system of government with queen

Elizabeth as Head of State for the first three and a half years. After that the country could become a republic with a President as Head of State, if the Parliament so desires" (17).

On May 26, 1966, Guyana became independent.

However, before the next election in December 1968, the union between the PNC and the UF "began to crack. "On the eve of the general elections, most of the UF ministers resigned from the coalition . . . This act did not however bring down the government since the PNC had successfully induced some members of the P.P.P. and U.F. to 'cross the floor' by which process it obtained an absolute majority. . . . The split [in the PNC/UF coalition] came in October 1968" (Lutchman, 238).

In December 1968 elections were again held and the People's National Congress gained a clear majority with 30 seats, the People's Progressive Party 19 seats and the United Force four seats. On the 23rd February 1970 Guyana became a Cooperative Republic within the Commonwealth.

Four parties contested the July 16, 1973 elections, Guyana's second since attaining political independence and first since becoming a Cooperative Republic. The PNC won 37 seats (a two-thirds majority), the PPP 14 seats and the Liberator Party (LP), a new name in the field, two seats. The LP led by Dr. Ganraj Kumar represented an elections merger with the United Force. The other party, a newcomer, The People's Democratic Movement (PDM) did not win any seats. PDM was led by Mr. Llewellyn John, a former PNC minister. (*Guyana Handbook 1974*, 15).

The PNC led by Forbes Burnham continued to be the party in power in government. In October 1980, Burnham was named the First Executive President and Dr. Ptolemy Reid was appointed Prime Minister in Burnham's place. Ptolemy Reid resigned the post of Prime Minister on 16 August, 1984 and was succeeded by Hugh Desmond Hoyte as first Vice President and Prime Minister. When Burnham died on August 6, 1985, Hoyte became President of the Republic until October 1992 when the PPP under Cheddi Jagan won the general elections and that party retained power until 2015. In 2015 A party for National Unity (APNU) and Alliance for Change (AFC) won the elections under the leadership of David Granger (now President) and Moses Nagamootoo (now Prime Minister).

In the interest of transparency, it is reported that

From December 1964 until his death in August 1985, Forbes Burnham ruled Guyana in an increasingly autocratic manner . . . During that timeframe, elections were viewed in Guyana and abroad as fraudulent. Human rights and civil liberties were suppressed, and two major political assassinations occurred . . . Agents of Burnham are widely believed to have been responsible for both deaths . . . [I]n 1985, Prime Minister Hugh Desmond Hoyte acceded to the presidency and was formally elected in the December 1985 national elections. Hoyte gradually reversed Burnham's policies, moving from state socialism and one-party control to a market economy and unrestricted freedom of the press and assembly. On October 5, 1992, a New National Assembly and regional councils were elected in the first Guyanese election since 1964 to be internationally recognized as free and fair. Cheddi Jagan was sworn in as President on October 9, 1992 (*Countries of the World and their Leaders Yearbook 2013*, 981).

To give some idea of the social state of affairs in Guyana beginning with the Burnham administration, I quote:

Following independence and with the help of substantial foreign aid, social benefits were provided to a broader section of the population, specifically in health, education, housing, road and bridge building, agriculture and rural development. During Forbes Burnham's last years, however, the government's attempts to build a socialist society, including banning importation of basic food stuffs, caused a massive emigration of skilled workers, and along with other economic factors, led to a significant decline in the overall quality of life in Guyana. (*Countries of the World and their Leaders Yearbook 2013*, 982).

# A Timeline of Dr. Reid's Life

Born May 08, 1918 in Dartmouth, Essequibo, then British Guiana (B.G.), Dr. Reid started primary school a year later than his peers. He passed the School Leaving Examination, but, in 1933, failed his first attempt at the Pupil Teachers' Appointment Examination. He later passed it after the flood of 1933.

| | |
|---|---|
| 1934 | At age 16, he became a pupil teacher at Dartmouth Anglican primary school. |
| 1939 | wrote the Teachers' Training College Entrance Examination and passed |
| 1939 -1941 | attended the Teachers' Training College |
| Sept. 1941 -49 | Trained teacher at Dartmouth school |
| 1941 – 1949 | Secretary of the Village Committee of Management |
| 1943 – 1949 | Secretary of the Essequibo Branch of B. G. Teachers' Association; founder and President of Dartmouth Eye Opener Consumers' Cooperative Society |
| 1949 – 1955 | Student of School of Veterinary Medicine at Tuskegee Institute, Alabama, U. S. |
| 1955 | visited Guyana, after Tuskegee. Married Ruth Chalmers |
| 1955 – 1957 | Meat Inspector in Canada; moved to Saskatoon in the Saskatchewan region |
| | At Milestone (prairies) did field veterinary work |

| | |
|---|---|
| 1957 – 1958 | Streatley-on-Thames England; student of Royal College of Veterinary Surgeons of London University; earned Doctor of Veterinary Medicine degree and qualified as Member of the Royal College of Veterinary Surgeons (MRCVS) |
| 1958 – 1964 | returned to B. G.; veterinary surgeon employed by Bookers McConnell (six years): became first vet appointed to Bookers' directorate- of the Kabawa Branch |
| 1959 | bought land in Bel Air; built a house |
| 1960 January | occupied house with a clinic in Bel Air |
| 1960 | invited by Burnham to stand as PNC candidate for Essequibo-Pomeroon |
| 1961 | bought land at Supply, E.B.D; moved permanently to Supply in 1967; failed election candidate for Essequibo-Pomeroon |
| 1962 - 1963 | turbulent years in B.G. politics |
| 1964 | entered government in December; appointed deputy leader of PNC (1964-1984) until retirement but kept the office until after 1985 elections; appointed first deputy Premier, Minister of Home Affairs; PNC – UF coalition |
| 1964 – 1966 | Minister of Home Affairs |
| May 26, 1966 | Guyana gains independence from Britain |
| 1967 | Minister of Trade (January -September) |
| 1967 | (Government restricted importation of fruits- December) D'Aguiar resigns as Minister of Finance, coalition remained intact to the end of the term (1968) |
| 1967 – 1970 | Minister of Finance |
| 1968 | PNC contested the elections as a single entity and won elections |
| 1970 | Guyana declared a Cooperative Republic |
| 1970 -1972 | Minister of Agriculture |

| | |
|---|---|
| 1972 – 1974 | Minister of Agriculture and National Development- He had planned to leave the government after the term was up in 1973 but thought he couldn't forsake the government in time of (oil) crisis. |
| 1974 | Declaration of Sophia; "promulgated the contentious doctrine of party paramountcy" ("The Last Hard Man", *Stabroek News*, Sept. 7, 2003) He volunteered (the only time) for General Secretary of the PNC thinking it would be only for one year. |
| 1974 – 1984 | General Secretary of PNC and Minister of National Development; functioned less as Minister and more as General Secretary. "The shocks of the petroleum crisis after 1973 had triggered worldwide instability, and Guyana's economy started the slow slide into stagnation." ("The Last Hard Man"). |
| Oct. 1980 | (Burnham became first Executive President) Reid appointed Prime Minister in Burnham's place |
| 6th Oct. 1980 – | 16 Aug. 1984 Prime Minister of Guyana |
| 1985-1992? | Special Adviser to the President (Hoyte) |
| 1997 | First wife, Ruth, died |
| ---------------- | Remarried childhood sweetheart, Marjorie Griffith, who died May, 2003 |
| Sept. 2, 2003 | Died quietly in his sleep at home in Atlantic Gardens |

# THE EARLY YEARS

Ptolemy Reid was born on May 8, 1918, in a small village called Dartmouth on the Essequibo Coast of then British Guiana. Dartmouth was formerly known as New Ground, which was bought by former slaves around 1856. There were 56 shareholders who organized and managed the village.

Herman Cecil Reid, Ptolemy's father, was a tall, serious man who journeyed from Devonshire Castle, a village about three miles away, to Dartmouth and took Flora Christina, Ptolemy's mother, as his wife. Flora was also known as Marion Monroe, fondly called by all "Auntie Marion." In those days, couples often delayed the act of marriage, so the two raised their family in what was then referred to as a "common law marriage." Ptolemy was the last of five children and the last born "out of wedlock." His parents married shortly after his birth.

At that time, the men at Dartmouth were generally peasant farmers and fishermen. They planted rice, plantains and cassava and fished. Women were usually homemakers. Ptolemy's father was a farmer and at some period a constable. He was also, notably, foreman of the burnt heap, a method used to make red brick to maintain the roads. Layers of green cruda wood were laid and alternated with mud fetched often by women. (The silt was taken from the trenches thus allowing for drainage). The wood was set alight and would burn a day or two to form red brick. The women pounded the brick and the men fetched the dirt in a donkey cart and "sheet it off" on the road and in potholes. Men called "rammers" used heavy poles to ram the mud in place to prevent it from blowing about in the dry weather. So, the heaps were burnt to change ordinary clay to a hard material known as red brick. Ptolemy's father had a contract with the government to supply this material. He employed a lot of villagers to work in the burnt heaps. One would work two or three days and stop, and another would then come on board. Since floods would often wash away the road, road maintenance went on continuously.

While Herman Cecil Reid lived, his family had a fair existence. At the time when Ptolemy should have begun school, the headmaster of the local school was W.E.A. Hart, Ptolemy's godfather. However, Ptolemy did not attend the school during Mr. Hart's tenure. As a small child, Ptolemy had long hair and when he went to the school, the class teacher refused to admit him with the long hair, and he had to return home. He did not go back to school until a year later when the new headmaster, Mr. Billy Chalmers, took over. When that happened, Ptolemy stood on a high bridge near the school and shouted, "I will now enter school because a new headmaster has come." (The bridge existed because Dartmouth was often flooded, and in those days, the people built high bridges under which boats could pass.) He agreed to have his hair cut and received a boiled egg as a concession. His hair was cut, parceled in a cloth and put away in a safe place.

Thus, Ptolemy started school, one year older than the normal age for the infant class. However, he did not stay long in Little ABC but soon moved on to Big ABC and then to First Standard. His school life continued, pleasant and peaceful, and he attended school regularly.

As Ptolemy grew, he probably followed the routine of the day for boys his age. They would go to the farm and cut grass for the cow and donkey. Nearly everyone owned a cow, donkey, or sheep. Everybody had a piece of land two to three miles long. The boys would go down to the farm with a grass knife, some travelling in small boats called corealls, and they would cut and fetch the grass to feed the animals. They would clean the chicken and/or pig pens and after bathing would go off to school. Likewise, at the end of the school day, some would return to the farm to cut grass or to reap mangoes, plantains and ground vegetables. Most people then were self-sufficient for staple foods. Some would go higher up the coast to sell their produce of mangoes, bananas and so on. Some transported their wares on a donkey cart while others did so on their heads and trekked barefooted to the point of sale.

As a small boy, Ptolemy enjoyed a pretty secure life under the protection of his father, but then tragedy struck. His father, Herman Cecil Reid, died from pneumonia in 1928 when Ptolemy was ten years old. Life changed fundamentally at his father's death. The children had to engage in economic activity. Just barely ten, Ptolemy found work in the burnt heaps and in the cane fields of the sugar estate, and he worked steadfastly in the family's ground provision plot and in a little patch where they grew rice. He was very helpful to his mother and worked so diligently that one neighbor referred to him as "a little toiler." He even dared to go to sea against the best wishes of his mother, who was terribly afraid of the sea.

Ptolemy spent some of his early life at sea as a fisherman, but not a regular fisherman. He used to keep an eye out to see when boats were working as they would, not too far from the village, about four miles out. Looking carefully, the small boys could see the masts of a "pinseine" boat about three to four miles away. The fishermen would pin a "seine" or net and the water would wash the fish into the net when the tide came in, and when it went out, the fish would be trapped. The boys would get on a catamaran and go on a "pillican." The catamaran was a long board which they lay on the mud. They sat with one knee on the board while the other foot propelled them off, and they skimmed over the mud carrying a small box and a cutlass in hand to help the fishermen kill and gather in the catch. The boys would then collect the small fish the fishermen discarded, called "pilikin" and take them home. Years later, Dr. Reid boasted that the catamaran formed his strong legs.

Fishing became an important job because, of all the economic ventures, it was the one that brought in the highest income. Many times, Ptolemy had to choose between going to school and going to get fish. Quite often the need for income over rode his desire for schooling. As the family's economic stability wavered, so did Ptolemy's attendance at school. So, Ptolemy no longer attended school regularly.

Speaking about his boyhood days, Dr. Reid said:

> I was a part of everything, part of a group . . . [I would] beat up, fight up. But after my father died, I had to be careful because my father wasn't there to defend me. For example, we had whips to beat up people and could be taken to court. I had to stop that. We had to leave home early in the morning – four or five o'clock. We had our bath in a trench; we put coconut oil on our heads and used

black sage to clean our teeth. We would get to school as fast as we could and had to respect the teachers. Licking [whipping] was the order of the day. I got licks for all kinds of things. Teachers were not certified; probably only the headmaster was.

I wore long hair to school on my first day and was sent home. In third standard, I had the first teacher who had passed school leaving – the first to pass school leaving in the village – I met that teacher. [That was the year my father died.] I played games "bat and ball" as we called cricket, rounders, tops, lick and pinch. And if there was fighting, I fought as well. I had problems with the girls at school. I remember interfering with a girl at school. Early [next] morning, I was passing in Better Success with coconuts on my head. The girl waited for me with a stick and gave me a good whipping. I had to run with the coconut on my head or it would break up.

We swam in the trench. We did catamaran in the mud for miles and miles. Pillicaning helped me to collect fish on the pin-seine boat. You got skin fish – now and again scale fish like Queriman- sometimes Gaulbecker, a large skin fish, sometimes Snook. Queriman used to run ashore. You were free to take it and go and sell it. Sometimes you made more money than the big men. When there was nothing else to do, we would go to Hampton Court on the cane field – at four or five o'clock in the morning hunting buffalo.

Once I went buffalo hunting and nearly got killed. I was the only one left on the ground. I ran for my life.

There were mangoes which we fetched on our heads from Dartmouth to Hampton Court, sometimes up to Anna Regina's market to sell, especially mangoes and coconuts. From the farm we learnt to make sweet and salt cassava bread.

My mother used to wash clothes, and I would carry the clean clothes to the Lorrys [a family in the neighborhood] and bring back the unwashed.

When I became a teacher, I gave up most of those tasks because I was studying for exams. Sometimes I would go fishing. I taught Sunday school, and the church used to have functions. I attended most of the weddings. The Father[priest] taught us to speak at weddings.

I joined the Boys Brigade, which was partly religious but was mainly physical training; . . I had a band; I always figured in school concerts – usually doing a recitation or in a school play." In third and fourth standards and especially in fifth standard, school inspectors, especially Mr. Dolphin, used to look for [him] for recitation. If he was absent the inspector would ask, "Where is the little boy?" Especially in sixth standard, the school master and his wife used to help him with [acquiring] books. {There were] just about three. Even if a book only cost a shilling, that was difficult to find to buy the book.

At the time of their father's death, Ptolemy's older twin sisters, Vivian and Clementina, had just passed the primary school-leaving examination. Then, successful students would normally seek employment as pupil teachers, that is untrained persons who assisted with instructions in the classroom. However, the school management decided they could only employ one of the girls. Vivian was employed around 1928. Just then, the country suffered economic problems, and there were massive retrenchments. So, after one year, Vivian lost her job. She never went back to teaching but did domestic work instead. When their father died, the three younger children – Vera, Rivers and Ptolemy – were still in school.

Rivers, who was a year older than Ptolemy, sat the school leaving examination and passed. A new examination, the Pupil Teachers Appointment Examination, had started, but Rivers could not take it because he was older than the stipulated age. The family had expected he would be a breadwinner, but he had to look for something, other than teaching, to do in the community. Although Ptolemy wanted to leave school, his mother was determined to live up to her promise to his father on his dying bed to keep the children in school until they took the School Leaving Examination. So, Ptolemy continued in school and sat and passed that examination.

As a boy, Ptolemy was serious; he did not play around with education as some other pupils did though he did like to "play ball," that is cricket. He was a great support to his mother and family, and his sisters, Clemmy and Vivian, who had both passed the school leaving examination, used to teach him at home. He was bright at school as was his peer, Annamunthdoo. He began to study for the Pupil Teachers Appointment Examination, but he failed that in 1933. That gave him the excuse to leave school totally. Only about 20 persons a year succeeded at the Pupil Teachers Examination, a highly selective examination. Unsuccessful at the examination, Ptolemy found no more reason to continue in school.

As fate would have it though, a great flood occurred in the country in 1933. At the best of times, however, Dartmouth used to flood. Now flood waters engulfed the roads three to four feet high. Houses flooded. The Reid's little shack, located far away on a dam called Middle Ark, became totally submerged. With other families, they sought refuge in the school in the latter part of 1933. Even after the waters had receded elsewhere in 1934, Dartmouth remained heavily inundated.

In January, the schoolmaster, who, during the disaster, lived in the school, decided that since Ptolemy also lived in the school, he would enter Ptolemy's name amongst the names of students who would take the Pupil Teachers Examination. Ptolemy agreed to this with the understanding that when the water receded, he would leave the school to engage in work. About a month before the examination, the water did recede and, as agreed, Ptolemy returned to work. But the headmaster, a kind man, told him to come back and join the class in the evenings whenever he could. Since Ptolemy's name had been entered for the examination, he attended some of the classes. He took the examination and resumed his non-school endeavors, forgetting about the examination.

One day, some time after Ptolemy had written the Pupil Teachers Examination and had returned to his money-earning activities, as he walked from the farm with a sheaf of grass on his head, an out-of-breath school teacher caught up with him. The teacher said that the headmaster wanted to see Ptolemy because the results of the examination had come from Hampton Court and he had passed. Another headmaster, Frank H. Russell, had come from Devonshire Castle, Hampton Court with the results and said he had come to Dartmouth to see the little fellow who had surpassed his own Hampton Court students. (In those days, Dartmouth did not have many successful students. Lucille Robinson, in 1925, became the first person from Dartmouth to pass the School Leaving Examination.) Both headmasters ecstatically congratulated Ptolemy.

Thereupon, the headmaster of Dartmouth School said he had a vacancy for someone to "act," that is work temporarily, the salary for this position being $4.00 a month. Ptolemy took the job and "acted" for some months. On September of that year, 1934, he got his first permanent appointment as a pupil teacher. At the same time, a change in the school administration occurred. The authorities transferred Dartmouth's Headmaster, Billy Chalmers, to St. Jude's School of Lichfield. A new headmaster, Joseph Walter Cox, came from Tapacuma Anglican School to Dartmouth School. Ptolemy started his first regular job as a teacher under Mr. Cox, who assigned Ptolemy to work in the infant class.

It so happened the morning Ptolemy began to teach, the manager, S.V. Kidd, visited the school. ["At that time practically all primary schools were managed by various Christian denominations under a system of 'dual control.' The government maintained the schools, which were built by the churches (later the government even built the schools), and also paid the salaries of the teachers, but the appointments of the teachers and the management of the schools were the responsibility of the Christian denominations" (Jagan, 19)]. The church usually appointed a manager, often a priest, to overlook the school. Mr. Cox informed Mr. Kidd that he had recommended the person who had passed the Pupil Teachers Examination for the teaching position. S.V. Kidd asked if the person was confirmed as an Anglican Church member, and he said that if he had known that the person, Ptolemy, wasn't, he would not have accepted the recommendation. However, the headmaster assured S.V. Kidd that the appointee was a candidate for confirmation, and that saved the day.

An interesting personality, the new schoolmaster, Joseph Walter Cox, wore to school a white suit every day and a white top hat that was called the "bug house." Always punctual for every occasion, he was on time for school routinely. He introduced a new arrangement and a new type of school discipline. He insisted that the school body should march on the grounds outside. They would mark time and enter the school in an orderly fashion, class by class. Whoever had control of the bell commanded the utmost respect from both staff and students. When the first bell rang in school, everyone would be quiet, and at the second bell, everyone stood up.

Of particular interest was Mr. Cox's organization for external examinations. No "extra lessons" were taught after formal school hours, but once students reached the highest level – sixth standard – they had to take the School Leaving Examination unless the parents absolutely disagreed. After school let out for the day, pupil teachers received afternoon lessons, so Ptolemy attended class after his students' dismissal. His day-to-day record keeping further reflected the headmaster's discipline. No compiling of records remained to be done after the end of the school year. On the last day, he signed the statistical sheet and dispatched the records to the Ministry of Education in the capital city of Georgetown.

The school at Dartmouth, under the foundation laid by Billy Harry Chalmers and the system instituted by Joseph Walter Cox, moved on to new heights. Students then commonly passed the School Leaving, Pupil Teachers and also the Government County Scholarship examinations. The last was a gateway into secondary school.

From the age of about sixteen, Ptolemy spent many of his holidays with relatives in Alexander Village, just outside of the capital city of Georgetown. His maternal aunt, Mary Franklin, lived there with her family, and Mary and Flora, Ptolemy's mother, were very close. Ptolemy enjoyed many happy times with his cousins. They used to stage "concerts" every night, singing and dancing, although Ptolemy couldn't dance; he would merely shake his shoulder and move on. He obviously looked forward to spending time with his relatives since he returned every holiday. On one such occasion, he contracted a fever while in Alexander Village, and his aunt, fearing he might die as an older brother of his had earlier died in her home, told him to return to Dartmouth. Children then being very obedient, he returned to his country home on the Essequibo, but as soon as he recovered, he came back to his cousins' house in Alexander village to finish out the holiday.

In those days, to rise socially, teaching was the most available option for a promising youth, especially one of a poor family and living in the rural areas of British Guiana.

All Ptolemy's experience as a pupil teacher took place under headmaster Joseph Walter Cox. He completed up to the fourth year of Pupil Teachers Examinations and wrote the Teachers Training College Entrance Examination in 1938. He did not, however, succeed at that time. At the end of the 1938 school year, the Ministry of Education transferred Mr. Cox and assigned a new headmaster to Dartmouth School.

The new headmaster, C.C. Bristol, came to Dartmouth from Leeds Anglican School on the Corentyne. He had a great interest in village affairs and in politics, both of the local area and in general. The school broadened out because of Mr. Bristol's interest in politics, with teachers taking part in the business of the village through village meetings.

At this time, Ptolemy decided to seek additional help with the Teachers Training College Entrance Examination, which would be held in April 1939. His friend Telford introduced him to Egbert Cornet, who held preparatory classes for the examination and had a record of turning out successful candidates. Egbert Cornet agreed to have Ptolemy join his Saturday classes.

The classes were held about ten miles from Dartmouth, which presented Ptolemy with the problem of transportation. He could not rely on the bus and, in any case, it ran at a different time than suited him. However, Telford came to the rescue and offered to transport Ptolemy on Telford's bicycle. So early every Saturday morning, Telford would tow Ptolemy on his bike from Dartmouth to Bush Lot, their destination, and back to Dartmouth in the evening.

Ptolemy wrote the examination with three other students in his class in 1939. Almost two months later, the Department of Education in Georgetown invited him to an interview for those who had passed. Even though the other students of Egbert Cornet's class had been attending his class longer, only Ptolemy of Cornet's four students that year succeeded. Three others from elsewhere on the Essequibo coast had also passed the examination, namely Cecil Williams from Anna Regina, and Ganesh and Moneram from Aurora School.

When the time for the interview came, Ptolemy travelled early that morning from Dartmouth to Georgetown. He did not know the city well.

In fact, he had visited Georgetown for the first time at the age of sixteen years. When he arrived there for the interview, he took a taxi to his relatives in nearby Alexander Village to change his clothing. He asked the taxi driver to return and take him to the Department of Education *for* three o'clock. He did not want to be late for his appointment, but as luck would have it, the taxi came back *at* three o'clock to Alexander Village, so Ptolemy got to the interview late. The other three young men had completed their interview when he arrived. The interviewer first asked Ptolemy the reason for his lateness, whereupon Ptolemy explained what had happened. The interviewer then enquired about his punctuality as a teacher. Ptolemy said he had only once arrived late in five years. The interview ended at that point. After he left the interview, he met the three other young men, who had waited for him, and they all wondered what would happen to him. However, he, with the others, later received a letter telling him to report to the training college in Georgetown for admission by a certain date.

With that letter, there came a long list of requirements for college. What he needed to purchase would cost $50.00. Ptolemy's family did not have that money, so they consulted a good friend of his late father, Simeon Benn, who said he did not have that money either, but he would put the matter to J.P. Clay and contact them after. J.P. Clay, presumably a well-established resident of Dartmouth, agreed to lend them the $50.00, without a guarantor, until Ptolemy finished college.

Apart from that issue, Ptolemy had just bought a bicycle for which he had to pay installments of $2.00. However, he would receive from the Teachers' Training College pocket money amounting to $2.50 a month. Since students had to each have a bicycle for college, Ptolemy went to the dealer from whom he had bought the bicycle and explained that he could not continue to pay the installments. The dealer, Sadar Mohamed of Danielstown, said that since Ptolemy had up until then kept up with paying the installments, he would defer the payments until after he completed college. At that point, he owed a balance of about $12.00. The dealer had made a great concession since the duration of college would be two years. With these difficulties resolved, Ptolemy went to Georgetown to live for the first time for an extended period of two years.

# At the Teachers' Training College

The teachers' college then formally called the Government Training Center had its male dormitory on Cowan Street and the female dormitory and lecture hall on Main Street. The day for the students began at 5:00 a.m. After getting out of bed, they prepared for physical activity at Eve Leary, a training ground north of the city, where Major Smith instructed them in physical exercise. When they returned to the dormitory, they dressed for class and had breakfast at about 7:30 a.m. The students would then go to the lecture hall on Main Street. They would return to Cowan Street for lunch, organized and headed by the resident tutor, the famous W.G. Griffith, the deputy head at Broad Street Government School and also a renowned cricketer. The evening meal was also formal, as, once more, they all ate together. After supper, the (male) students went back to the lecture hall on Main Street for evening study. They would return to the dormitory between 9:30 and 10:00 p.m. for "lights out," though some had secret lamps that they used for further reading.

When he arrived in Georgetown, Ptolemy had little knowledge of the surroundings. He first of all looked for the nearest Anglican church, which happened to be Christ Church. Like his fellow batch mates, that is students who entered college in the same class/year as he, he benifited from living together, for the first time, with persons from most regions of the country. The students had come from the West Coast of British Guiana (B.G.), from the East Coast, from Corentyne. None of his peers that year, however, had originated from the hinterland.

The first holiday, Christmas 1939, soon arrived. Ptolemy went back to Dartmouth for the period. Before he had left for college, he had had to visit each household in the village to let them know he was leaving for college. Similarly, on his return for holiday, he had to visit everyone. He showed them the college uniform, including a major part, the celebrated cork hat, nicknamed the "bug house."

While in Georgetown, Ptolemy experienced new methods of teaching. He did teaching practice in a number of schools, but he spent his longest period of practice at Christ Church School, where he taught for one month. When students of the College were going on teaching practice, it was customary for the principal of the College to read out the list of schools where practice would take place, and students would volunteer for a school.

Unfamiliar with the schools in Georgetown, Ptolemy volunteered for Christ Church School. He attended Christ Church for worship and knew of the adjacent school. He also encouraged Cecil Williams, who sat near him at College, to choose Christ Church. After the session with the principal, some of the students who had become acquainted with Ptolemy tried to persuade him to go to the College principal and change his elected school. They intimated that, for some reason, Christ Church School did not usually get student teachers; it was only a formality to include the school on the list. They felt certain Ptolemy could easily be granted a change. However, Ptolemy decided he would stick with his choice, as did Cecil Williams.

For teaching practice at Christ Church School, the school's headmaster assigned one section of standard four students to Ptolemy and one section of fifth standard students to Cecil Williams. After their first day there, it became clear why teacher training college students avoided Christ Church School. Ptolemy pondered how he would make out with these students because they did not seem to have come to school to learn. They refused to listen, and they had no exercise books or pencils.

The student teachers could not flog or administer corporal punishment (then common), and they could not send students too often to the headmaster, then C. Walker, who alone could flog their students. However, the headmaster would often simply send back to class students referred to him for discipline.

Ptolemy decided he had to find a way to get paper and pencils for the students, and, instead of sending them for flogging, he made some of them responsible for the performance of their peers who sat in the same bench. This approach seemed to have some success.

Usually, the principal of the teachers' college visited the teachers on practice, as did a female instructor, Miss Harris. However, she never, in two weeks, visited them. When the principal of the College visited Ptolemy after two weeks, he said to Ptolemy, "Reid, would you like to go to another school?"

Ptolemy said, "No, sir."

The principal said, "Your companion is going to Broad Street Government School tomorrow. If you want, you can go there."

Ptolemy continued for the third week at Christ Church School doing what he felt would help the students to be interested. When the principal of the Government Training Center returned at the end of the third week, he said he thought Ptolemy was doing well and that the school's headmaster had given him a good oral report concerning the learning he saw taking place in Ptolemy's section of standard four. At the end of the fourth week, the headmaster of Christ Church asked Ptolemy to consider accepting an appointment at the school when his training was over. Ptolemy told him that he could not make such a promise and that he had, as was expected, to return to St. Barnabas School in Dartmouth.

After Ptolemy's stint at Christ Church School, it became compulsory for students from the College to do teaching practice at that school.

Ptolemy himself did teaching practice at other schools, including Harts Congregational, Wortmanville Roman Catholic and Broad Street Government schools. At each one, he learned a great deal.

During the holidays, while he was at college, Ptolemy did not always go immediately back to Dartmouth, for his old schoolmaster, B. Harry Chalmers, always welcomed him at the school of which he was headmaster, at Lichfield, West Coast Berbice. Usually, the College closed long before regular school, and Ptolemy was always excited to go and do additional teaching practice at Lichfield, where he would be given tasks to help prepare the students for the School Leaving and Pupil Teachers Examinations. He found great joy in this activity. He would spend the first part of the holidays at Lichfield and the second part at St. Barnabas School, Dartmouth.

Ptolemy graduated from the teachers' college in 1941, after a period of two years there, with the grade one, class one teacher's certificate, and he received his assignment to St. Barnabas. It was not the usual practice then for students to be sent back to the same school from which they had come when they entered college. But in Ptolemy's case, at the time of his leaving St. Barnabas for college, a commitment had been made to the parish priest that he would return to the Dartmouth school. Thus, he alone of his graduating class returned to the same school he had left upon entering college.

The sad incident of the death of one of his batch mates, Randolph Goodluck, occurred while they were at college. Goodluck slept in a bed next to Ptolemy's in the dormitory, and the night he became ill, Ptolemy first alerted others that someone was not well. Goodluck went to the hospital, and the students visited him daily. When they saw him at mid-week, he assured them that he would be out of the hospital that Saturday. However, Goodluck died on Friday night and was indeed out on Saturday, but not at his own volition; rather Death had been the decider. None of the students had thought that Goodluck was so ill that he would die. Ptolemy's was one of the few batches where someone died while at college.

This death led to a critical incident, one of two incidents for which Ptolemy might have been expelled but for the understanding of those with whom he had to deal.

After Randolph Goodluck's death, his parents came to collect his belongings, but no one could find his football boots. The principal decided, and actually said to the class, that someone must have stolen the boots. Ptolemy objected to the accusation. He stood up and said he did not believe any of the students would have taken the boots. Whereupon the principal replied, "Okay, Reid, you find the boots."

Ptolemy replied, "Whether I find them or not, I do not believe any student has stolen them."

The students were quite concerned about this matter. After consulting with each other, they decided the boots must be at the shoemaker's. They called the janitor of the College and asked him to go to the shoemaker, but they advised him not to ask if the boots were there. Instead, he should say he had come to collect them.

While the janitor was gone on the errand, the students waited anxiously in the College yard for his return. At last they saw him turning the corner on his bicycle waving the boots in the air. Imagine the joy of the students!

The next day, the principal asked the student representative about the boots. The rep said they had been found. During this discourse, Ptolemy kept his head down; he did not look up. The principal remarked, "Reid, you were right."

Ptolemy said, "Thank you, sir," and the matter rested there.

Another incident that might have led to Ptolemy's expulsion occurred. During the first term, he experienced some eye problems and did not attend all classes, especially the science class, which Beavis, a master from Queen's College, the top boys' high school in the country, conducted. Even though he did not attend all the classes, Ptolemy looked at the notes and kept up with the class' progress. Test time arrived, and Beavis administered a term test, at which, according to the rule, only questions relating to matters addressed during the term could be assigned. When the instructor wrote the science questions on the blackboard, Ptolemy noticed that some pertained to topics not addressed during the term. He stood up and informed the teacher of this discrepancy, to which Beavis responded, "You must take the test," and resumed what he was doing. When he lifted his head again, Beavis saw Ptolemy standing and asked if he was not taking the test. Ptolemy responded that he would not take it until Beavis removed two of the questions.

Beavis then asked one of the better students for his notebook and looked through it carefully. He, thereupon, went to the board and erased the two questions. Nonetheless, the other students thought that Beavis would get even with Ptolemy in grading his answers. Beavis, however, marked Ptolemy's paper without prejudice to the incident, and no disciplinary steps were taken against Ptolemy.

# RETURN TO DARTMOUTH

In September 1941, Ptolemy replaced the first trained teacher sent to Dartmouth, Basil McGowan, who had been his senior in college. Basil McGowan spent one year at Dartmouth, where he taught third standard. When Ptolemy got to Dartmouth school, the headmaster assigned him to the class that had been McGowan's; most of the students were promoted to fourth standard. Ptolemy learned that the year before this had been the rowdiest class in the school. The first day of class, he noticed this group behaved less well than the other classes, especially the smaller students of the class. He suspected that the older ones had put them up to misbehaving. The second day, one of the older students who seemed to be a ring leader acted up and Ptolemy took him out of the classroom and flogged him. The other students responded in amazement that this particular student was disciplined, and, after that, Ptolemy had no more trouble with them even though some of these students were as tall as Ptolemy and possibly physically stronger. They and Ptolemy became good friends.

C.C. Bristol, the same headmaster Ptolemy had left at Dartmouth when he entered college, gave Ptolemy free reign to operate as a teacher. Ptolemy used the project method he had learned at college. He spent a lot of time outside of the school building with his class. They did physical training and even activities he was not good at, such as art and singing songs.

Ptolemy involved himself in many extracurricular activities. He taught Sunday school, sometimes in the church nearby, and he organized the youth group. C.C. Bristol, ever interested in village affairs, promptly named Ptolemy to the position of secretary of the village committee. Though there was no local authority in the village, there was a committee.

There was plenty to do, in Dartmouth, not only during the day but in the evening. C.C. Bristol was rightly called the "village politician," and so the two men worked together.

Ptolemy moved as teacher from fourth standard to fifth and sixth standards with the same group of children. He also bore responsibility for children taking external examinations: School Leaving, Pupil Teachers Appointment, Pupil Teachers and even the Government County Scholarship examinations. However, all the staff played a part in helping with these examinations. The school moved from a reputation of fair and very fair to excellent, both in record-keeping and in instructions. The students became famous for doing well and passing the external examinations.

From 1941-1949, Ptolemy participated in many kinds of activity. He organized a class for teachers on the weekend, and teachers came from miles away for these classes. Those who came to teach at Dartmouth without certification gained certificates before they left as the headmaster insisted on teachers receiving certification.

Apart from the work he did in teaching, Ptolemy worked in other areas in the village. In 1947, teachers engaged in registering voters for the 1947 election, the first election in the country, after World War II.

Guyana had a chequered constitutional history. From the Dutch had been handed down the Court of Policy and the Combined Court which put political and economic power into the hands of the sugar planters. When, in the 1920s, local professionals and businessmen won elected seats and the Popular Party made inroads so it seemed that power might pass into the hands of the nationals, this prospect "so alarmed the plantocracy that in 1928, the Constitution had been changed by the substitution of the Crown Colony system which effectively denied power to the representatives of the people . . . The franchise was severely restricted, hedged in by qualifications as to income, property and literacy, thus denying the majority of the people the right to vote and representation" (Jagan, 64-65).

The new constitution of 1928 which made British Guiana a crown colony removed all power from the elected element in the Legislature and transferred it to the Governor and the Executive Council (Bacchus, 55). This 1928 Constitution, with minor modifications, remained in force until 1943. Elections had been postponed – there were no elections from

1938 – 1947- even though "the old legislature had been constituted in 1935" and elections should have been held every five years. The war was given as an excuse for the postponement (Jai Narine Singh, 12; Jagan, 65).

"In 1943 a new constitution had been granted with a Legislative Council of 4 'ex officio' members including the Governor, 7 nominated non-official and 14 elected members" (Jagan, 65), thus giving the elected members a clear majority in the new Legislative Assembly even though executive power remained in the hands of the Governor and civil service (Bacchus, 55).

The Labour Party, comprised of a group of individuals from the top of society rather than representative of the masses, was one of the main contestants in the 1947 elections. Dr. Jagan and his wife were independents in the Georgetown constituencies rivalled by candidates supported by the Catholic Church. The League of Colored People (LCP) and the British Guiana East Indian Association (BGEIA) were also dominant on the political horizon. According to Jagan, C.V. Wight "shared the limelight of the planters' rule" (67).

Many candidates contested the Pomeroon/Essequibo constituency, one being C.V. Wight. Although this was the first time Ptolemy would vote, under the direction of C.C. Bristol, he had to register voters. One teacher registered voters in Dartmouth, while Ptolemy registered persons from the nearby area of Better Success to New Road. Whereas Guianese of African heritage resided in Dartmouth, non-African Guianese, mainly those of East Indian ancestry, populated the area from Better Success to New Road. Ptolemy found it exciting visiting homes, not just to look for children, but to find out particulars about the parents.

C.V. Wight enjoyed the support of the people of Dartmouth. The headmaster was a functionary involved in the elections, and many of the people keenly took part in doing whatever they could to get C.V. Wight elected.

David Maraj, A.A. Pawn and Sintoman Ajit were among the other candidates contesting the electoral seat. It fell to Ptolemy to persuade people in his community and in Pomeroon/Essequibo to vote for C.V. Wight. Specifically, he had to monitor the polling stations at Dartmouth on election day. He would monitor from outside the polling station. He did a lot of campaigning running up to the elections and got into some serious difficulties because he took it upon himself to be a platform speaker, even though he received a warning against such a risk. It was a risk because of the antagonism of the opposing candidates.

One of the candidates sent a messenger to him to urge him to stay away from campaigning, and the candidate would pay his monthly salary. Ptolemy, offended at receiving such an offer, replied that he was not prepared to accept money he did not earn, and, besides, money was not a consideration in the election. The people wanted a proper school, for whenever it rained heavily, the rain would pour in and there would be no classes. Moreover, the village flooded when it rained and at high tide, the roads flooded. The villagers had decided that in the 1947 elections, they were voting for a good school, for poldering of the village, and for a sluice- a structure that would enable proper water control. The people had clearly explained these conditions to C.V. Wight and had established a committee to work to bring these plans to fruition. Ptolemy informed the messenger of these plans and that no one else, apart from C. V. Wight, could at that point in the campaign assume these responsibilities. Ptolemy also told the messenger to reassure the candidate who had sent him that, as was customary, he could use the school for his political meeting.

The following day, a Sunday, Ptolemy learned that there was a meeting at the other end of the village. He went there and found this same candidate campaigning. Ptolemy had a confrontation with the candidate in which he told the candidate that he had come too late on the scene and that he would get no votes from Dartmouth. The candidate talked about his prestige and how he had met the queen, but Ptolemy said only the improvement of the village and the school mattered. He said that now that he had encountered this candidate, he would work all the harder to ensure he was not elected. The candidate left the meeting in a rage and reported to everyone, including the manager of the school, what an upstart they had as a teacher at Dartmouth School. At the elections, that candidate, by mistake, got one vote in Dartmouth, and he lost his deposit (which presumably candidates running for elections had to pay) as Ptolemy had predicted. It was discovered that he had merely been trying to split the vote.

At that time, trained teachers taught for two years after graduation from college and, if recommended at the end of that period, they would be given permanent appointments. Ptolemy had just completed his probationary period and had left Dartmouth to go on holiday in Berbice. He had spent a few days in Georgetown and was on the train on his way to West Coast Berbice when a policeman at the train station approached him hurriedly and gave him a telegram. The telegram said that his mother had been taken to the hospital. He had left her in fair health, although she was known to be a diabetic.

Ptolemy returned to Dartmouth to find out his mother had had a flare-up of diabetes because of an injury, and her condition was critical. She could still speak and recognize people, but she indicated that she did not think she would survive. Ptolemy always thought that his mother, in trying to care for her children, had worked herself to death. The last morning he visited her in the hospital, he left thinking there was still a flicker of hope that she might survive, but she died the next day. Her body was taken promptly to be prepared for burial.

Just then, a synod was taking place in Georgetown, and all the lay readers of the church at Dartmouth had gone to the capital city. Ptolemy was the only lay reader left in the village. He remembered his mother, some years before, telling her friends, when he was reading in church for the first time, that now they had somebody from the village to read for them when they died. So, although everyone thought that it would be difficult for him to carry on the service for her funeral, he decided to do it, having gathered strength from what his mother had said earlier.

Ptolemy's mother was buried in the Hampton Court church yard, and every time he visited the Essequibo Coast after that, especially around May, Ptolemy took a wreath to the tomb. A year later, he lost one of his older sisters, who also died almost suddenly from diabetes. She had left two children in his care. They later bore children of their own and moved abroad.

Certain matters in the village demanded a lot of attention. One was surveying the village in the process of getting proper titles for the shareholders. The land had never been legally distributed after its purchase by the former slaves. In the effort to properly drain and irrigate the village, the shareholders had to obtain proper titles. Some people had squatted on land, especially in the front of the village. Ptolemy was at that time secretary of the village, and it was the August holiday season. Strangely, no information had reached Dartmouth about the surveying, and Ptolemy had travelled to Georgetown, where he made his usual call in to see the representative in the legislative council for Essequibo/Pomeroon, Mr. C.V. Wight. Mr. Wight asked if Ptolemy knew the surveyor would be visiting Dartmouth the following day. Ptolemy said he did not know that and doubted that any of the villagers knew. Mr. Wight remarked that notices should have been posted in the post offices.

Ptolemy travelled back to Dartmouth the next day, and on the boat at Vreed-en-Hoop, a port on the route from Georgetown to the Essequibo coast, he encountered the surveyor, conspicuous with his equipment, also making his way to Dartmouth. Ptolemy approached the surveyor and let him know that the villagers had not received news of his visit. The surveyor said it had been published in the gazette, but, of course, in those days, nobody in Dartmouth read the gazette. Ptolemy told the surveyor that he was the village secretary and would render every assistance in the undertaking. The surveyor said that all the villagers who claimed lands would have to present a written application to him before they would get any consideration whatsoever.

When he landed on the Essequibo Coast, Ptolemy went to the shop of George Annamunthodoo and learned that the notice of the surveying had indeed arrived there. However, the villagers had not been informed because of the assumption that they would be on the spot in the village when the time came for the surveying. On arriving at Dartmouth, Ptolemy sent the children to alert their parents that they would have to make an application for land. This resulted in general confusion. However, the villagers mobilized about a dozen senior school children, who received a copy of the application, and they wrote the application for about 100 claimants. They worked all through the afternoon and into the evening.

Ptolemy was then still a bachelor. At the end of the task, the Annamunthodoo family, close friends of his, invited him to supper. There, he was told that the family had applied to claim a portion of land an old man was occupying behind the property they were claiming to have bought. Ptolemy told them they could not claim the additional portion, not only because somebody was living on it, but because it did not belong to them. They said they would not be removing the person; he would continue to live there until he died. Ptolemy said that was not acceptable.

The next day, work continued with the surveyor, but the Annamunthodoo family did not withdraw their application. Ptolemy again went to the family home for supper, since the person who cooked for him was away. Once again, the subject of the Annamunthodoo's application came up in discussion. Ptolemy once again said they could not make such an application, and, moreover, a few others who were attempting to do the same thing of claiming disputed territory should withdraw their applications. Annamunthodoo considered that his proposed claim would be a difficult matter to deal with even in court, and he withdrew the application. The two other persons who had made similarly questionable claims also withdrew their applications, and the surveying proceeded as peacefully as could be hoped for. Obtaining legal title to their land was important in the life of the villagers in Dartmouth because, for the majority of them, a piece of land, however small, gave them their only means of income from the village.

Once the people of Dartmouth began acquiring proper ownership of the land, because of the generally poor treatment they endured, they decided to begin a cooperative movement. After a lot of studies, those in the forefront began discussions with the villagers and encouraged them to contribute and raise a certain sum of money with the intention that when they acquired that sum, they would decide on a venture that could be undertaken and that would give the villagers some more dignity and self-respect.

The villagers spent many Sundays collecting 24 cents – a shilling – per home so each shareholder would have a share of $5.04 in whatever venture they chose. When they had accumulated approximately $1,000.00, the villagers held a public meeting, and all agreed to the proposal, from the floor, to invest in a consumer's cooperative enterprise. They, therefore, started preparing a building for a shop.

Just about that time, a cooperative adviser named Cheeseman had come from England to British Guiana. He advised that their choice of enterprise was one of the difficult cooperatives to manage, but if they were determined to follow the rules, he would support them. He organized the bookkeeping operation so simply that, within a few hours, a school teacher had learned how to keep the records. Before the shop opened, however, Cheeseman left the country, and Gordon from Jamaica succeeded him.

He, too, thought theirs was a difficult endeavor, but since they had started, he encouraged them to move along.

The organizers kept several meetings to inform the people of Dartmouth how the cooperative would operate and the kind of discipline it would require. Soon the doors of the coop shop opened. Immediately, treatment in the private shops changed dramatically, with the quiet competition between the old shops and the new one. Ptolemy left the shop doing profitable business in 1949, but the difficulties that arose became more and more monumental, and the cooperative officers, not fully committed to the cause joined the organizers in not enforcing one of the important rules, that all sales would be in cash. That error marred the workings of the cooperative, and after about eight years of operation, the cooperative was discontinued. The building became the village office and remained part of the community facilities.

From that time on, Ptolemy came to the conclusion that he would not engage in politics as a means of livelihood. He wrote that off. There were a few other things he had written off as a means of livelihood, and those included law and the priesthood. He resisted all encouragement to get into those fields.

# PTOLEMY, THE TEACHER

Ptolemy earned quite a reputation as a teacher at St. Barnabas School in Dartmouth. Pupils faced the prospect of entering his class with trepidation. In those days, when corporal punishment was accepted as a form of discipline, he was said to have a heavy hand. One former student said, "He han' heavy bad."

Another declared, "When he lash you, was a lash. He strong."

The pupils nicknamed the leather he flogged with "Vashti" after the first pupil who felt its weight. Although he was strict, he was not cruel.

The children of Dartmouth could not loiter on the street. If Ptolemy was out on the street at night and met one of the pupils, the next day, in school, he would check on that person, who had better not make any error in his/her school work. Ptolemy was so revered that when people saw him approaching, especially if something was amiss, they would begin to disperse one by one. The school children steered clear of him.

When an event was to take place in the village that would be the time that "teacher Ptolo" would assign the most homework to his pupils. He used to say the event was big people's affair, and pupils shouldn't attend. If he saw them there, they would have to report to him in school the following day. Should they dare to complain to their parents about his behavior, they got a double dose of punishment. The parents respected him and did not object to Ptolemy's discipline.

The pupils could gauze "teacher Ptolo's" mood and responses from how he dressed. Particularly if he wore a black tie, that was going to be a bad week. Teacher Ptolo would be in a severe mood. No one could slip up. Regarding sporting events, if the school's team lost a competition, they had to explain to him the reason for their defeat, and it had better be a justifiable reason.

But the best day for the pupils in Ptolemy's class was Friday. They would have a spelling bee and quiz on what they learned. With him, subjects like geography turned out to be practical experiences, such as making a journey to Georgetown, or they would have to act out scenes. He liked to see the pupils do drawings. For example, in nature study, they had to label drawings, and more than notes he gave credit for maps and other physical representations. This love for drawings held true even in Ptolemy's Sunday school teaching. He would draw the roads to heaven and hell with a big gulf between them. The road to hell was extremely wide, and "if you see the people dancing" on that road. On the other hand, the road to heaven was "narrow narrow."

Ptolemy liked to teach poetry. His pupils had to memorize long poems and could recite many of them several years later. They included "Will" by I. Van Sertima, "If" by Rudyard Kipling, and "Casa Blanca." As one student said, "They were powerful poems . . . 'I am the monarch of all I survey'."

The impact that Ptolemy had on the community led his pupils to testify that they had "passed through Ptolo's school." They felt that that was a mark of achievement- that once they had had Ptolemy as a teacher they could do anything; they had had a sound foundation. But there were other teachers at St. Barnabas- among them Messrs. Barth, Noble, Glasgow and Ellis- who deserved credit as good teachers.

# On to Tuskegee

In 1949, the British Guiana government expressed the need for persons to study in fields other than law and medicine. Ptolemy opted to study agriculture, specifically veterinary science. In 1949, he left British Guiana and started studies at Tuskegee Institute, later Tuskegee University. He left for what he thought was a four-year course, but when he arrived there, he discovered it would be a six-year enterprise. He was still at the time a bachelor.

As a pupil he had read *Up from Slavery* by Booker T. Washington for one of his examinations and had been impressed by that work and the work of George Washington Carver. He had made up his mind that if he ever had the chance to study overseas, he would like to be a student of their school. Therefore, he applied to Tuskegee Institute in Alabama, U.S.A. and was accepted.

The first problem Ptolemy encountered in trying to realize his ambition to study abroad was acquiring foreign exchange, that is equivalent U.S. currency for Guyana dollars. Ptolemy went to the public buildings to apply for foreign exchange, but even though he had gained admission to Tuskegee, the officials there did not think he was qualified to study abroad and did not grant him the foreign exchange.

During this period, he had kept in touch with C.V. Wight, the representative in the legislative council for the Pomeroon/Essequibo district in which Ptolemy lived, and he dropped by his office to give him an update of the progress being made in the development projects in the village. C.V. Wight asked him how his plans to study abroad were coming along, and Ptolemy told him he was about to relinquish the idea since he could not get foreign currency. Wight told Ptolemy to meet him at the public buildings at 1:00 p.m. that day and he would see what could be done to help Ptolemy. Ptolemy arrived there long before the time, and when Wight arrived, they approached the official who had denied Ptolemy the exchange. The man eventually approved U.S. $500.00 dollars, which he calculated as sufficient for one year of study abroad, although Ptolemy would have liked to have had a bigger allowance. With the help of several calls from Wight, Ptolemy readily acquired his medical papers and visa and returned home the next day with all of the documents he needed to travel.

He left Dartmouth School with very short notice to the headmaster and, especially, to the pupils because of the difficulties he faced in trying to make departure arrangements. He had applied for leave some months before, but the Ministry of Education officials had not granted it. He had to deal with A.A. Bannister, the acting principal at the Department of Education, concerning this matter. Bannister told Ptolemy that he had not approved his leave because he did not think Ptolemy should be going to study in the U.S., but rather, he should go to nearby Trinidad. Ptolemy told him he already had a date for departure settled and he would be proceeding abroad. Subsequently, the Ministry approved three months' leave.

Ptolemy had a memorable experience the first day he arrived in the U.S. He was supposed to be met by a friend at the airport in New York, but after his plane had left Atkinson Airport in British Guiana, it ran into bad weather and was diverted to Miami. By the time Ptolemy arrived in New York, his friend had left the airport because he had to go to work. However, at the desk of the arrival lounge, he left the address of a hotel where he had booked lodgings for Ptolemy. When Ptolemy finally arrived in New York, he answered his page and got the message left for him. The airport staff helped him into a taxi and sent him on his way to the hotel.

Ptolemy got to the hotel he had been directed to, but, there, the receptionist told him there was no vacant room for him. Nonetheless, the hotel personnel were willing to help him find a place for the evening. They contacted the YMCA and got him accommodations there. Ptolemy left a message at the hotel telling his friend where to find him. His friend arrived at the YMCA about midnight and told Ptolemy that, in being denied lodging at the hotel, he had experienced his first taste of segregation and discrimination in the U.S. For that reason, his friend tried to dissuade him from going to school in the southern state of Alabama, but Ptolemy replied that he had travelled specifically to go to the South and had made all arrangements for that. Whatever the conditions, he would travel there the next day or, at most, he would spend one day in New York. He did spend a day in New York and went to the train station the morning after.

At the train station, Ptolemy asked to purchase a ticket to Chehaw, but the attendant argued there was no such place. Ptolemy insisted that there must be and suggested that the attendant ask another colleague. The place was identified and Ptolemy got his ticket. He travelled as far as Washington, and when he tried to board the train again, he was told he could not go into the same carriage and that he needed to go and get a registration. This registration seemed to ensure that blacks and whites did not travel together, for when he looked into a carriage other than the one in which he found himself, he saw only whites there. He asked for an explanation and learned that as you travelled to the south, there was segregation not only on the train, but on buses also.

When Ptolemy disembarked at his stop at Chehaw, there was no one in sight and he thought he remembered a similar situation having occurred in *Up from* Slavery. After a while, a taxi drove up and the driver asked Ptolemy if he was going to Tuskegee. He had been sent to transport any student who might have arrived late. When Ptolemy got to Tuskegee, welcoming students took charge of him, and they assigned him to a dormitory.

Registration was then in progress, but the freshmen, the first year students, had already registered and only juniors and seniors, third and fourth year students, were in the line awaiting their turn. However, Ptolemy joined the line. When it was his turn to register, he and the clerk were having difficulty understanding each other. Then Ptolemy felt a tap on his shoulder and the person asked if he was from British Guiana because he said he was from Trinidad and could always recognize an accent from the Caribbean and from Guiana. They made acquaintance, and Ptolemy learned that the young man was a junior named Montague Oliver. He offered to do the registration for Ptolemy and later took him to meet some of the Guianese and West Indian students.

Then, there were only three other Guianese students at Tuskegee: Joseph Smart, Cedric Thompson, and Francis Morgan. Ptolemy made four. Years later, not long before 1988, when as a Guyana government official, he visited Tuskegee to make arrangements so students could pursue overseas education vigorously, Ptolemy thought it significant to find over 100 Guianese students at Tuskegee Institute. After that first arrival at the Institute, he soon got acquainted with all the foreign students, then totaling in the twenties and coming from many parts of the world, including Africa.

Contrary to his expectations, Ptolemy discovered that he had been registered in the pre-veterinary course extending over two years. Having never attended secondary school in Guiana, he had not studied science subjects and could not therefore be accepted into veterinary school. He profited from those two preparatory years during which he did some subjects he thought were not directly related to his major, veterinary science. He did all kinds of extracurricular activities and courses, including a course in typing. He also attended the Episcopal program Sunday school.

On campus, there was a chapel, and the college required students to attend services there twice on Sunday, at 11:00 a.m. and 6:00 p.m. Since he was Episcopalian, Ptolemy did not have to attend many of the chapel activities, except the evening program. Before long, some students took exception to chapel attendance, especially since they had to march to chapel. Up to when Ptolemy left Tuskegee, the college had not abandoned chapel attendance, although it was still being debated. Some years later, the college did discontinue marching and the compulsory requirement.

Much learning, however, took place in the chapel itself, for the chapel was a center of cultural activities of all kinds. Some of the great artists of the day visited there, and outstanding preachers addressed the students. The Baptist pastor who resided nearby became a great friend to Ptolemy over the years.

Once a year, Tuskegee selected a student to present a message for the chapel program. This was an honor that was hotly contested. A student could only enjoy this privilege once during his time at Tuskegee, and many people considered selection to perform this function quite an achievement. In his second year there, the college gave Ptolemy the opportunity to write the student message and deliver it after it was vetted.

Of particular interest was Ptolemy's experience with the Episcopal club. He became president of the club in the second term of his first year. At one point in time, Auburn University, a white institution in

Auburn, Alabama invited Tuskegee's Episcopal club to attend an activity on its campus. University and college students who were members of the Episcopal church were gathering together from all over the South for a weekend retreat. As the Tuskegee students were preparing to leave the next day, some students from Auburn arrived with the message that they should not make the journey, but only the foreign students who were Episcopalian should attend. The Tuskegee group objected to the change as being discriminatory, since the University had addressed the original invitation to the entire club. Auburn University gave no further explanation for the change, but through his efforts to find out more, Ptolemy later learned that the community at Auburn had raised such serious objections that the bishop had to intervene and had made the decision that the University should withdraw Tuskegee's invitation to the conference.

Four years later, when Ptolemy was still president of the club, Auburn University extended another invitation To Tuskegee and the Episcopal club decided to attend if all went well. This time, there was no cancellation message, and the Tuskegee club members went to the conference. They were welcomed, and they spent the weekend in all kinds of activities. At the evaluation session at the closing of that conference, most people said that the event had gone well and had been useful. Some commented on how inspiring it was to see negroes and whites together at the communion rail of the Auburn Church.

When it came time for the Tuskegee students to comment, Ptolemy represented their club. He remarked that notwithstanding all that the participants had said and done, theirs was a difficult situation to accept because what they had experienced seemed superficial, since, once the conference participants separated to go their own way, they could not sit on the same seats on the public transportation. He said further that the U.S. government and people had to bear responsibility for that situation and that they were not morally strong enough to give leadership to the world if they continued to practice the kind of segregation evident everywhere, most especially in the South, but also in the North. He recounted the experiences he had had at the hotel in 1949.

When he transferred from the school of pre-veterinary medicine to that of veterinary medicine, Ptolemy began once again as a freshman. The School of Veterinary Medicine was situated about a mile from the main campus, and it consumed all the time of its students. They could no longer engage in many of the activities they had participated in during the pre-veterinary studies. This first veterinary year was a year for "pops." "Pops" was the name then given to little quizzes that were unannounced but detailed enough to cause one to be expelled for not being able to keep up the pace. One of the professors was actually called "Pops" because so many freshmen used to be popped out of the school in their first, second or third term. Ptolemy's class of 1951 had started with 17 students, and, at graduation, only seven remained.

Sophomore year was also difficult. Students had to wrestle with disciplines like physiology and bacteriology. Whereas in the first year, anatomy did the popping out, in the second year, physiology and bacteriology popped out the unfortunate students.

For much of the time while at Tuskegee, Ptolemy had to find means of earning. The first Christmas of 1949, he found himself left with only U.S. $1.00 from what he had been allowed in foreign exchange from British Guiana. His roommate at Tuskegee was a Jamaican named Arthur Reid who advised Ptolemy to go to the Dean of Men and explain his situation. Ptolemy had already acquired permission to work during the holidays and was able to get an outdoor job helping to keep the campus clean. Some of the other fellows thought he should try to get a job in the building, probably in the library, since it was in the cold December month. However, Ptolemy said that he would take the job that would give him the most money. He took his first job and learned within the space of an hour to push a wheelbarrow, to shovel debris and help other workers to keep the place tidy. It turned out to be great fun for him. He made several good friends. Many of them thought he should cease studying and continue doing that work.

It was clear that Ptolemy would need to continue working part-time and, after consulting with the Dean, he got permission to work part-time on a continual basis on the campus. He, however, spent his summers working off campus. The first summer, he decided that he could not go with the other foreign students to work on the tobacco farms in Connecticut because he would not earn enough to take him through school for the year. So he negotiated other areas for work. He began his first summer vacation in Reno, Nevada. He traveled in the bus for four days and four nights and experienced some of the segregation in practice. Travelling on a bus, blacks were more tightly squeezed into the back as more and more whites entered in the front. They would eventually have to stand, both men and women, even those with babies in their arms. Once in Reno, it proved difficult to get a job, but he did many things such as painting, woodwork and carpentry.

Then Ptolemy was referred to the railway station to seek employment. The manager there was not unwilling to take him on, but he gave him a task difficult for anyone new to the U.S. A vacancy for a red cap, which is a porter who took luggage on and off the train, did exist. However, Ptolemy was told that to be employed, he had to know the train stations from New York to San Francisco. The manager showed him a board with a list of stations between New York and San Francisco at which the train would stop. He told Ptolemy that when he knew that list by memory in the particular order, he could return for a job. Determined to find work, Ptolemy spent the night memorizing the list. The next day, when he returned to the manager, the manager thought that Ptolemy had misunderstood his instructions, and he was surprised to find that Ptolemy could recite the names of all the stations in the prescribed order. The manager said he had not expected Ptolemy to return, but since he had memorized the list, he would find something for him to do. So it was that Ptolemy worked as a red cap that summer.

Passengers on the train paid ten cents per piece of luggage to get it tagged, but, in addition to this specific remuneration, they often paid far more. Sometimes they paid as much as one dollar, depending on how they felt and the kind of conversation that they engaged in with Ptolemy as they walked between the train and the train station. Ptolemy did a lucrative business that summer and determined to return the next summer, but that did not happen since he found other means of employment.

The station manager, however, did his best to have Ptolemy stay on the job as a red cap for his career, even though they had had at least one serious argument. It happened on that occasion that Ptolemy had taken luggage off the train, and a passenger complained that she was missing a fur coat. As the red cap, Ptolemy was responsible for the luggage, but he firmly maintained that he had not received a fur coat. The manager could not appreciate Ptolemy's stance in opposition to the passenger, who was assumed to be right.

Ptolemy suggested that the manager check whether the fur coat had been left at the station from which the passenger had travelled. When the manager inquired, he found that indeed, the coat had been left at the previous station. The manager was impressed by Ptolemy's courage in arguing so strongly, and he was offered a permanent job. The manager contended that there was more money to be made doing the job as a red cap than in studying veterinary medicine. To convince him further, the chief of the red caps travelled from San Francisco to persuade Ptolemy to stay on. Nonetheless, at the end of the summer, Ptolemy left and never returned to Reno.

The following summer, Ptolemy went to work in the steel mills in Gary, Indiana, where he spent his second summer in the U.S. There, he also did well financially; both summers, he returned to college with practically enough money for his financial needs for the entire year, and with the help of additional part-time work on campus he made it through the years.

On their first time at the steel mills, the group of Tuskegee students had experienced some difficulty being employed, even though some of them had obtained permission to work while others were permanent residents and could legitimately be employed. They had argued their case successfully, resulting not only in their eventual employment at the mills, but they had also been invited to return the next year.

As the third summer approached, Ptolemy decided not to go straight away to the steel mills, since he and other students had been assured of jobs there. The same student who had assisted him with his initial registration at Tuskegee, Montague Oliver, had been introduced to some friends at Alabama State University and had decided to get married. Thus, they spent some time travelling to the wedding and missed the first two weeks of work. When they finally arrived in Gary, Ptolemy and the other students worked for two weeks, after which there was a national steel strike. This was a very delicate period, for they could not be employed. The young men searched for something to do. Ptolemy found a job in a restaurant. Too anxious and busy to ask what the pay would be, he threw himself into the job, but after working a fortnight, the pay was so small that he wondered why he had worked at all. So, Ptolemy gave up that job and resumed looking for work. He did not find any work for many weeks. Finally, the strike ended about one month before the new college term was to begin.

After work resumed, the boss at the steel mills allowed the students to work long hours. Ptolemy worked 16 hours a day, and since overtime was double pay, he was able to accumulate a tolerable amount as the end of the summer approached. But then, a letter came to him from Tuskegee, inviting him to assist with the orientation of new students. That necessitated his returning to the campus at least two weeks before the term began. Ptolemy discussed the offer with his good friend, Montague Oliver, who assured him that such an offer meant he would have his tuition for the year paid by the college.

Ptolemy left his summer job and returned to Tuskegee where he participated in seminars and received instructions on how to assist students during orientation. He joined the team involved in that process, and before classes began, he was given an award which excluded him from paying school fees for the year. That was the first time since he started college that he did not have to worry about a meal card.

Ptolemy entered the sophomore year and went on to the junior year of college. Usually, students from the veterinary school were selected to stay on in the summer and assist in the clinic. It was customary for juniors to volunteer for this. However, one summer, too few juniors volunteered and sophomores were requested to fill in. Ptolemy volunteered and was given accommodation in what was called "the barn," which was a facility reserved for veterinary students specifically selected to reside there. Those who lived there had their school fees reduced, having to pay for meals only.

At the end of the summer, the dean gave Ptolemy permission to continue living in the barn, even though it was normally reserved for juniors. So he spent both his junior and senior years living in the barn. That gave him the added advantage of witnessing all the surgical cases that took place in the evenings and the opportunity to attend all the calls around the veterinary school. He was present for all of them. Then came the last summer at Tuskegee when most of the surgical work in the senior year was done. Once again, the professors gave Ptolemy full reign to practice the skills.

Senior year was relatively easy to complete as one prepared for graduation. For graduation at Tuskegee, Ptolemy was selected to give the valedictory speech at the closing exercises. Of the four prizes awarded by the veterinary school, he had earned three of them; one for the best student at the clinic, another for the student of veterinary medicine who did the most to promote the veterinary school on campus, and the third for research on poultry pathology. That was the first occasion that one student had won 75 percent of all the prizes of the veterinary school.

During senior year, Ptolemy contemplated returning home to British Guiana. Early in the senior year, he applied to that country's Department of Agriculture for a position as a veterinary surgeon, but he got no response. It happened that the British High Commissioner based in the U.S. was making a round of visits to schools that students from British colonies were attending. In his interview with the High Commissioner, Ptolemy informed him that although he had applied for a job in British Guiana, he had received no reply. Two weeks later, Ptolemy got a formal application form in the mail, which he promptly completed and mailed to British Guiana. He heard nothing further.

Graduation came and went and, still on campus, Ptolemy decided to look elsewhere for work. He applied to the veterinary division of the Canadian government's Ministry of Agriculture and within a week, got an offer of a position. Nonetheless, Ptolemy decided to return to Guiana before taking up an appointment elsewhere. He therefore informed the Canadian government of his plan and proceeded to British Guiana. That was in 1955.

Soon after he arrived in British Guiana, Ptolemy got married to his old school mate from Dartmouth School, Ruth Chalmers. Her father was at one time the headmaster of the school at Dartmouth. (It was at Headmaster Chalmer's following school assignment at Lichfield, West Coast Berbice that Ptolemy had worked during the summers of his years at the teacher training college in Guiana.) Ptolemy then set about preparing to travel to Canada when one day, he met his former batch mate from the teachers training college, Basil Owen, who was then employed by the Department of Agriculture. Basil Owen asked Ptolemy when he would start work in the Department. When Ptolemy explained that the Department had not offered him a job, Owen said he felt sure that Ptolemy had been approved for a position. He promised to check into the matter and did so.

Subsequently, Gavin Kennard, Acting Director of Agriculture, invited Ptolemy to an interview. When he inquired what had happened to the reply of a job offer that should have been sent to Ptolemy, the piece of mail was found in one of the clerk's cubicle. The clerk had not mailed it because a change in the salary for the position was pending, and he was awaiting that change before mailing the offer.

Despite being persuaded by all to accept the position in Guiana, Ptolemy decided that since he had already accepted the position in Canada, he would go there. He also had an interview with the colonial secretary, who laid out the terms of employment. These stated that to be employed on a permanent basis, British qualification was necessary. The British Guiana government would offer Ptolemy a position on the condition that he would agree to attend a British school to acquire the qualification that would give him permanent status. Ptolemy informed the colonial secretary that apart from having accepted a position in Canada, because he had not received a timely reply from British Guiana (B.G.), he was not prepared to accept that condition, although he hoped to return to B.G. some day.

# Interlude in Canada

After his wedding, Ptolemy journeyed to Canada. It was warm when he left British Guiana, but when he reached his destination, the town of Saskatoon in the Saskatchewan region, where he had acquired an appointment as a meat inspector, he had to search for warm clothing; it felt so cold.

The veterinarian in charge of the meat packing plant welcomed him at the train station in Saskatoon and made accommodation arrangements for him and his wife. He indicated that he would call for Ptolemy to escort him for his first appearance on the job. Saskatoon is a town in the prairies. Summers were very hot and the winters long and cold. It was an area known for serious blizzards, but Ptolemy had made up his mind to stay on the job.

Everywhere on the streets, people inquired what he was doing in that part of the world. It was so rare to see any negro on the street that when two negroes encountered each other, they happily made each other's acquaintance. A lot of the white folks, when they met him and engaged in conversation, would try to determine what type of work he was doing in Saskatoon. They would first suppose that he was a porter. Some wanted to know if he was a boxer, or thirdly, an entertainer. After a while, many of them gave up trying to guess what his job was or, Ptolemy suspected, they might have found out where this strange individual was working. At Saskatoon, he was closely attached to the church as well, and his first and only child was born in this town about ten months after Ptolemy's marriage.

At his workplace, the meat packing plant, Ptolemy had to go through a learning period, despite the fact that he had studied and graduated. He had to learn the intricacies of the job in a practical way. A senior veterinary officer, a man from Yugoslavia working in Canada, supervised and trained him. The training period, before he could go on the killing floor alone, normally lasted six weeks.

Ptolemy had to oversee live animals to make sure they were alive when slaughtered. He did supervision of slaughtering and examination of the carcass and the entrails before they could be passed and stamped for the market. He supervised the processing of meat of all kinds. He was the only non-white working in that plant at the time, and the plant provided him with every facility needed to perform well.

After a couple of weeks, Laobe, his immediate supervisor in the plant, reported that he had successfully completed tutoring and guiding Ptolemy. He was satisfied that Ptolemy was capable of working on the floor after those two weeks. However, since the normal training period was six weeks, whenever the man in charge came on the floor he would himself do his own checking on Ptolemy, whose first experience on the floor alone came after three weeks of training. Ptolemy's quick adjustment to his task was probably due to his having done plenty of practical work, including in the area of meat inspection, while he studied at Tuskegee. Soon he was documenting the post-mortem reports and sending them through the system and on to the head office at Ottawa. The feedback that came from the veterinarian in charge in Ottawa was always highly complementary.

Ptolemy enjoyed doing meat inspection, but his reason for being abroad was not only to make money for personal use at that time, but also to go to a British school. He thought that to succeed with his goal, he had to get involved in field work and field practice, even in that cold country.

According to the information he got from the veterinarian from Yugoslavia and also one from the Ukraine, he had to pass the provincial board examination and become a full member of the Saskatoon Veterinary Association. Then, he would be given a license to practice. They indicated that the examination was difficult to pass. Ptolemy listened very carefully to this information. Their training facility was good enough to give him a copy of ten years worth of questions from the board examinations, which he kept and used as if they were a bible. His workmates kept saying that if he took the examination, he would not pass it, but Ptolemy was determined to go through with it. So he did, as the first year of his meat inspection position was coming to an end. He took the provincial board examination about April of that year.

Usually, the examination results would be announced at the veterinary association's annual meeting, wherever in Canada that took place. The candidates who had succeeded would be invited to the meeting. Ptolemy waited to hear the results, but August came and went, and the association had its annual meeting, but no results were announced. All the veterinarians in the plant were interested to know what was going on. One of them had once taken the examination and had passed, but he could not stand up to the rigors of field practice in that cold country. They all wanted to know what Ptolemy would do if he passed. He had pretty much given up hope of hearing anything when, one day, he received a letter inviting him to send his membership fee so he could get a certificate for practice. It was a strange development, and no one could explain why the examination results were handled in this manner on this particular occasion. As soon as he got his certificate, Ptolemy decided to apply for work in Milestone, a district some 500 miles away, but still in Saskatchewan.

Before beginning practice, Ptolemy needed to discuss with the head of the veterinary division of the University of Saskatchewan the field work that was required to be done by the government of Canada – mainly testing and vaccination of large animals. Thus, he attended an interview with the head of the veterinary division of the University. During the interview, Ptolemy mentioned that in coming to Canada, he had hoped to get the opportunity to eventually go to a school in England to obtain British qualifications so he could work in British Guiana.

The head of the veterinary division expressed the opinion that Ptolemy needed no further qualifications, but Ptolemy informed him that the practical situation required it and that he had applied to schools in England. The division head said he would give some support to the application because he did not think Ptolemy needed to spend two years at any school to obtain membership of the Royal College of Veterinary Surgeons. He further added that Ptolemy had attained the opportunity to practice because of the work he had done; otherwise, he would not have passed the examination. The head of the veterinary division went on to explain that the examination results had not been announced on that occasion because there was discomfort over the results. In the marking of the papers, to maintain anonymity, the officials had assigned numbers, replacing candidates' names, to the answers. As the questions were marked, one number kept earning the highest grade and everyone was curious to know who the person was, but they did not divulge the identity of the person but kept the anonymity until all of the results were in. Then, they discovered that the man who placed second earned a grade in the seventies, whereas Ptolemy scored well near to full marks for every question.

About this situation, Ptolemy believed that because he was a foreigner and a "nigger," he was not announced as the winner at the Association convention; his performance was not recorded in writing. If the [examiners] had known he was black, he wouldn't have attained the first position in the ratings. However, one man supported him by writing to get him off one year of study in England. Ptolemy also believed that, in Britain, when they saw he was black, he was required to complete two years' worth of studies. He did two years of work in one year, whereas others- the Europeans- did only one year's work.

Ptolemy went on to do practical work on the prairies in Canada for a while and had a wonderful experience working in the field in the community of Milestone in Saskatchewan. There, he met some of the kindest people. They willingly paid whatever price he charged for his service, and he worked with the pharmaceutical and instrument sections that gave him full cooperation in every area.

Nonetheless, Ptolemy still needed to go to England to obtain the British qualification required for employment as a veterinary surgeon in British Guiana. He wrote the British counsel in London, and he gained admission to do a course there that would be completed in one year, instead of the normal two years. Ptolemy set out for London from Milestone, Canada, the last post where he worked in private practice doing field veterinary work. He left the prairies in 1957 with his wife and his son, the latter just about one year old. They travelled by road from Milestone across the prairies and on to Montreal, where Ptolemy disposed of his car. His wife and son returned home to British Guiana, and a few days after, he boarded a ship to London.

# Study in London

Ptolemy arrived at Southampton, England, and was welcomed by those responsible for student affairs from London University. He was booked into a hotel in London and later, a room was found for him where it was thought he would reside for at least one year. However, within a week, he learned that the major part of his studies for the veterinary course would take place at the field station at Streatley-on-Thames. Hence, he had to find new residence as near as possible to Streatley-on-Thames. He left London and at first stayed in a hotel where there were a number of other foreign students, mainly from India, Pakistan and Europe. Some days later, he was able to get accommodation in the home of a two-person family. Their daughter had recently married, leaving them with a vacant room, which they kindly offered Ptolemy. The home was two to three miles from Streatley-on-Thames and Ptolemy made the daily journey by bus to the veterinary outstation and joined the class there.

There were probably about 20 odd students, including English students, in the class, all of whom were striving to achieve membership in the Royal Veterinary College. Although he had already completed a course in veterinary medicine, Ptolemy joined the class of final-year students. Though they were just doing their final year, he was doing a combination of third year and final year courses. Every weekend, Ptolemy had to travel to London to do laboratory work to cover the third-year laboratory curriculum. Some of the students thought this arrangement was not fair to Ptolemy, but he contended that since he had come to London specifically to do two years' work over the period of a year, he was not complaining. Getting back and forth between London and Streatley-on-Thames week by week sometimes proved to be quite exciting.

The content of the course was fairly familiar because it was work Ptolemy had already covered as Tuskegee Institute. The main difference was that while his peers were doing only final year examinations, Ptolemy had to answer questions covering two years' work. There was great difficulty making adjustments to accommodate this arrangement, but eventually, adjustments were made, and Ptolemy was able to take the required examinations.

It would be well to mention one or two of the important experiences that happened during the course. On the prairies, Ptolemy had done a fair amount of large animal practice, as well as small animal practice. The concentration of work in London was on small animals but included a fair amount of meat inspection and visitation of farms. Ptolemy had worked in Canada before getting into private practice as a meat inspector at a Saskatoon meat packaging plant where animals were inspected in large numbers. Carcasses came through the line in great quantities, and the inspector had no chance of repeating anything. He had to do the incision right, to identify the lymph nodes and things of that nature. Thus, over that period, Ptolemy had become fairly efficient at meat inspection.

In his meat inspection class in London, an incident occurred where the professor indicated to the students that he had not found the lymph node on a carcass under examination by the class. Ptolemy whispered to the little group with whom he was working that the lymph node must be there if the butcher had not removed it. The professor overheard the whisper, which had not been intended for his ears, and challenged Ptolemy to find the lymph node if he thought it was still there. Ptolemy took the knife and the hood, promptly incised the carcass and pulled out the lymph node. When the class was over, the professor asked Ptolemy how he was able to find the lymph node. Ptolemy explained that he had to do that – finding lymph nodes – to make a living, and when carcasses were passing through the production line, one could not miss anything. Moreover, unless one was proficient at identifying those lymph nodes, one could not properly qualify to become a meat inspector, and thus the process was routine to him. The professor then said that Ptolemy need not attend any more meat inspection classes, and so he was relieved of that one requirement.

After that incident, the same professor became Ptolemy's close friend. So it was that Ptolemy learned from him that there had been much discussion about whether Ptolemy should be allowed to do two years' work in one year. The council had finally agreed to it, and so he was accepted on trial, but it did not appear that such an arrangement would ever again be repeated. The professor also remarked that unless Ptolemy was careful, he would not qualify at the coming examinations.

Ptolemy concentrated most of his time on the work before him, and he wrote the examination, which consisted of written, oral and practical tests. Concerning the theoretical part – the written part of the examination – the same professor whispered to Ptolemy that he had scored the second highest points in the group, and he confided that he no longer feared whether Ptolemy would pass. Ptolemy was encouraged to receive this information about his results in the written test.

In the practical section of the examination, he was confronted with the very professor who had argued strongly against having Ptolemy in the course. That professor was responsible for the practical test. Ptolemy was given the assignment to do the castration of a horse. He had done much of this type of work in practice, but at Tuskegee Institute; as a final year student, he had been exposed to much of the surgery that had to be done during the course. Castration was one of the operations he had done even as a student at Tuskegee. When he had completed the castration in the examination, the British professor asked how he was able to accomplish the task so well. Ptolemy informed the professor that he used to practice veterinary medicine in the prairies of Canada and castration was routine there.

When this examination was concluded, the students sat in the lobby and waited for the results. Everybody was tense. At last, the professor came into the lobby and started to write the names of those who had passed. The second name he wrote was Ptolemy's. Some of the students did not see their names, and there was moaning, especially among those who were foreign students. The English students, however, took their failure in stride. If their names didn't appear, it did not matter too seriously to them. They would repeat the examination the next time, whereas those who came from overseas were not at all happy to repeat the examination.

After the completion of the examination and the publication of the results, the students entertained the professors at the pub, which was the customary practice. The professor who had doubted that Ptolemy would pass commented that he was afraid that within a few months, Ptolemy would collapse. To that Ptolemy responded that time would tell, but he was feeling good at the moment.

Thereafter, Ptolemy left Streatley-on-Thames and decided to spend time in London seeking opportunities to return to British Guiana. He did not receive any response to the application he made to Guiana, so he tried elsewhere, but he did not want to return to the prairies.

At that time in London, there was some upheaval at Nottingham Hill and members of the government of British Guiana, along with those of the Caribbean governments, had gone there to make representation. Ptolemy attended one of those meetings, at the end of which he, with other Guianese present, had the opportunity to meet the leader of the Guianese delegation. Ptolemy told this person that he had completed the requirements and attained the qualification of Member of the Royal College of Veterinary Surgeons (MRCVS) and that he was hoping to return to British Guiana but had been told by the colonial office there was no vacancy. The person encouraged Ptolemy to make an application to him. Ptolemy said he could not do that because if there was no vacancy, there was no vacancy, and he did not follow up that proposition.

Ptolemy made job applications elsewhere, including to Ghana and Nigeria, and he was interviewed by both places and received offers of assignments. Nothing was concluded because he had in mind that if he was to give service, it must be first to home in British Guiana, secondly, to Tuskegee Institute, and then elsewhere. Accordingly, he had also written to Tuskegee, informing them that he was available for work, since he had no appointment from home. Before long, Ptolemy received a response from Tuskegee, and the dean of the School of Veterinary Medicine arranged for him to get the necessary documents, including a permanent visa, as he was offered the appointment as assistant professor in large animal surgery. He was asked to report for work at the earliest possible opportunity. Hence, Ptolemy purchased a ticket to travel to the United States, booked in his luggage and had a date fixed for the journey.

However, Ptolemy still had a few more days in London, and on one of his visits to the West Indian Center, he met a few of the fellows that he had known over the years. Among them was Henry Thomas, who was then an employee with Bookers Sugar Estates in British Guiana and was on a special course in London. Henry Thomas informed Ptolemy that he had learned, a few days earlier, that a veterinarian who had been employed with Bookers had died and, most likely, the company would need somebody to fill the vacancy. Thomas asked Ptolemy if he was interested in that position, to which Ptolemy responded by relating his situation that he had his ticket in hand to travel to the U.S. and his luggage booked in. Thus, it would be difficult to do anything different at that moment. Thomas proposed that if Ptolemy cared to visit Bucklersbury House, headquarters of Bookers McConnell, the next morning, Thomas would accompany Ptolemy. Ptolemy said he had no objection to the visit as long as his situation was clearly understood. They did make the visit and found that it was true that the veterinarian had died, but the public relations officer at Bookers McConnell said he could not make Ptolemy a job offer because the office in British Guiana had not asked for that to be done. Ptolemy noted that he had arrangements in place to travel to the U.S. and if it would take a long time to make inquiries about this position, he did not have that time.

As the two men were about to bid farewell to the public relations officer, he remarked that he could send a cable to British Guiana. It would take a day or two for a reply and he would contact Ptolemy.

The next day, Ptolemy received a call from the officer, who said he had received a reply and wanted Ptolemy to return for an interview. At the interview, Ptolemy was told that Bookers was willing to accept him for the job vacancy at home if he was in a position to accept it. Ptolemy said he would reconsider his options, and he gave that serious thought during the evening. The next day, Ptolemy reported back that he would cancel his arrangement with Tuskegee Institute and accept the job at home.

Ptolemy was then told that there was a director from Bookers Sugar Estates in Guiana visiting in London, and the director had asked to meet with Ptolemy before the latter left for British Guiana. By then, Ptolemy had reported to the dean at Tuskegee his changed circumstances and that he felt obligated to return to Guiana now that the opportunity had arisen. The dean understood the situation well and was sympathetic even though all arrangements had been made for his appointment to Tuskegee.

Ptolemy did revisit the Bookers McConnell headquarters and spent a long time in discussion with the visiting director, during which Ptolemy got the impression that they did not believe he wanted to get back to

British Guiana. They offered to mail his luggage for him and asked how he would travel to Guiana. Ptolemy said he would go by plane taking light luggage. Only then did the officials seem convinced that he was intent on returning home. Ptolemy later found out that the director and others at the headquarters were unsure of his commitment because they had not discussed salary. Ptolemy did not think it necessary to ask about salary; he simply wanted to go home.

# Return Home

Within another day, Ptolemy was on a plane to British Guiana. An officer of Bookers Sugar Estates met him at the airport and welcomed him back to Guiana saying that all were looking forward to seeing him. As they drove to Georgetown the Bookers officer was making excuses about the poor condition of the road, but Ptolemy eventually told him there was no need to talk about that because he was from British Guiana and knew it was an undeveloped country. Furthermore, Ptolemy said that even in the developed countries, not all the roads were good highways. When they got to Georgetown, he checked into a hotel arranged by Bookers since most of Ptolemy's relatives were not expecting his return due to the sudden change in his plans. When he turned up to visit some of his relatives, they received Ptolemy with great amazement because the last they had heard of him was that he would be returning to the United States to work there. However, Ptolemy had been able to send a cable in advance to his wife, and she traveled to Georgetown to meet him after his arrival.

Meanwhile, the officials at Bookers advised him to stay in the hotel for two weeks while they prepared accommodation for him at Lamaha and Cummings Streets. They were refurnishing the house before he moved in. The company told him they would provide a chauffeur to take him around Georgetown and any place he wanted to go so that he would be acquainted with the town. He signed an agreement to work for a period of three years. Remuneration was agreed to and fixed, and a car was put at his disposal while he remained at the hotel. Everything that he had seen so far was so well organized that Ptolemy thought this must be a very efficient establishment.

There was just one awkward situation in that period. One day, a chauffeur was to take him into the town so he could get a local licence to drive. The chauffeur was to pick up Ptolemy at nine o'clock, but by 9:30, he had not come. Ptolemy called the company to find out what had happened and was told that the chauffeur had been to the hotel at about nine o'clock and had not found Ptolemy. However, he would return. When the chauffeur did arrive, Ptolemy asked if he was the person who had earlier knocked on his door but then said he was at the wrong place. The man said he was the one, and he had returned to the company saying he did not find the person he was sent for. Later, as they drove in the town, the chauffeur explained that though he had seen Ptolemy on his first arrival at the hotel room, he did not think that Bookers had employed a negro, since they had never before had a negro veterinarian on the sugar estates. (At that time, Bookers being a British company employed mainly British European expatriates in upper level/supervisory positions). The chauffeur apologized. Ptolemy said he understood, and they got on with the business at hand.

Soon Ptolemy was taken on a tour of the sugar estates by the very director whom he had met in London, Mr. Eccles. They went in a small plane to all the estates reaching as far as Skeldon in the Berbice region, and Ptolemy was introduced to the managers and some of the senior people as the new veterinarian surgeon. They were told he was not going to begin work for another week or so. The tour was very informative, and the director told him that he would probably be traveling from estate to estate as they were travelling then- by plane. They also visited Kabawa Ranch, which was to become a very familiar place for much of the work he had to do. At the end of two weeks, Ptolemy moved from the hotel and took up residence at Lamaha and Cummings Streets, which he learned, afterwards, was where the previous veterinary surgeon had resided.

# Experiences as a Veterinary Surgeon

Ptolemy got acquainted with the local veterinarians, including Dr. McWatt, Dr. Bird and Dr. Brazen. Some of them had indicated that he should not have accepted the salary he did since it was less than that of the former veterinarian. Ptolemy told them that the previous veterinarian had more experience whereas he was a newcomer, just out of school, even though he had practiced two years on the prairies.

He continued his work and organized training courses for the animal attendants. Some people did not think the courses necessary, but Ptolemy insisted that if they were to work together, then he and the attendants must get to know one another better, and the best way for him to know the attendants was to have a course or many courses arranged from time to time. It was finally agreed upon, so for the first time, a course was organized for animal attendants on Bookers Sugar Estates. The first animal attendants' course went well and other courses were planned.

There was initially an insistence that artificial insemination should not be included in the animal attendants' course as some of those workers had not had any formal education. After some persuasion, however, the Ministry of Agriculture agreed to make some instructors of artificial insemination available. By the end of the course, some of the animal attendants had become very efficient at artificial insemination to the extent that one participant was sent to Florida for further training and left a record at the institution there of being a very proficient inseminator. Of course, he had to be proficient because this was the attendant who was in charge of Bookers dairy at Bel Air, which had over two hundred dairy animals.

Some general rules of understanding needed to be established for the creation of a positive working environment. For instance, it was customary that when one visited the estate, one had to report first to the administrative manager, regardless of the urgency of the visit. Ptolemy made an agreement that when he was on an urgent call, he would inform the manager as quickly as possible by whatever means available, but not always by physically presenting himself. He said he would let the administrator know that he was on the estate and when his task was finished, he would visit the manager. The officials agreed to some of these new arrangements that had to be made if they were to work amicably together.

Shortly after assuming his post, Ptolemy became a member of the local veterinary association and in other ways assimilated into the society.

He travelled often all around the estates routinely every month. Apart from that, he visited on call or made visits that he personally arranged to see what was going on. He was invited to use a small plane for his travels, but he preferred travelling by road since that gave him the opportunity to visit with some of the people he knew over the years, especially his fellow teachers at some of the schools along the coast. Moreover, on his return journeys, he sometimes stopped at villages and had conversations with the people; this he enjoyed fully.

He also arranged with Bookers to carry on private practice. In fact, that was part of the arrangement he had made in London before he had agreed to return home – that he would be allowed to do private practice. He, thus, set up a clinic at Lamaha Street where he did his private practice.

Further, the Royal Society for the Prevention of Cruelty to Animals (RSPCA) asked Ptolemy to assist them at their clinic on Robb Street, as the former veterinarian used to do. So he took on that task as well. He used to go there twice a week. The first afternoon of his service, there were three or four people who came to see the veterinarian, but before long, he was dealing with 20 to 30 clients every afternoon. He did all kinds of tasks at the clinic, and he really enjoyed the work there. People did not pay for the service, but the RSPCA paid him what was considered some of the expenses involved in the practice. From that practice, his own practice at his residence benefitted from time to time, and he employed some of the new surgical exercises not then used in British Guiana. Hence, he engaged in a very challenging tour of service between the private clients, Bookers Sugar Estates and the RSPCA clinic. Ptolemy stayed with Bookers for some six years, and he resigned from that job when he entered the government in December 1964.

While he was a veterinary officer with Bookers, Ptolemy received promotion to the directorate of the Kabawa Ranch. He learned that that was the first time Bookers Sugar Estates Ltd had appointed a veterinarian as a director. His overall working situation was one that was full of rewards, not only monetary. His private practice involved work not only at the clinic but took him to the farms and the homes of people; he did all kinds of interesting work.

There was one particularly memorable experience he never forgot – an incident with a cow in the La Penitence area. Ptolemy was at the time living at Bel Air. He had acquired his own property; he had purchased a lot of land at Bel Air in 1959 and had built a house, with a clinic on the ground floor, which he occupied from January 1960. Early one morning, two children came to the Bel Air facility. They had walked the considerable distance from La Penitence, and they asked Ptolemy to visit their home in La Penitence for they had a cow that had taken ill and could not get up. Ptolemy took them in his car to their home. There, the mother told him that the cow had stopped producing milk, which was their only source of income. The children's father was in the gold fields (in the interior of the country), and they were not hearing from him. The mother asked Ptolemy to treat the cow and wait for payment at a later date. Ptolemy said he would do his best.

It happened to be a simple case of illness, and within a short time the cow stood up and started to eat. The family expressed such joy at the cow's recovery that Ptolemy would never forget the incident. A home that was sad was made so happy because a cow that they thought was dying was full of life again. The change in the face of the mother, in the big ones, the little ones – they sparkled with life. The mother then began offering Ptolemy all manner of gifts in gratitude. Did he want some eggs? Would he take a chicken? But Ptolemy refused all and told her she need not bother to pay him, instead he would consider the case as an introduction to his practice. When the father returned from the gold fields, he and his wife visited Ptolemy and again offered payment, and again Ptolemy refused to take anything. He didn't expect them to pay. Somebody had to pay. Those who could pay paid for those who couldn't in Saskatchewan and in

Guyana. "This," Dr. Reid said, "is what President's College* is all about. A lot of them can pay, but some can't."

While working on the prairies, Ptolemy used to hope for the day when he would practice in British Guiana and would get the opportunity to do work of that type whether there was payment or not. That incident with the cow was one of the outstanding examples of what he had looked forward to doing at home.

There was another notable case where a client called on Ptolemy to investigate the death of an ox that had worked late into the night but was found dead the following morning. All those involved were quite certain that some malicious person had poisoned the ox or maltreated it in some wicked way. Ptolemy could not reach a conclusion as to the cause of death without a post mortem, although the others concerned did not believe the post mortem would mean anything. However, he did the post mortem and discovered to everyone's surprise that an old nail was lodged in the animal's heart. As a matter of fact, that organ had very little tissue that was of any use. Everyone wondered how that ox had been able to live over a long period with a heart in bits and pieces from severe inflammatory conditions. They also wondered how a nail could reach the heart. Ptolemy explained to them that it was not an unusual condition in ruination as a material, like metal, taken into the stomach can move across from the stomach to the heart and destroy it after a period of months.

Yet another case of great interest occurred when a fellow practitioner summoned Ptolemy because that practitioner had a case of a bitch that was in serious condition. They decided that they would have to perform an operation to save the animal. Nonetheless, the veterinarian who was in charge decided to continue to treat the bitch without any operation. The next day, the animal died. They performed a post mortem which showed that it was one of the usual illnesses that would end in that kind of death unless an operation was carried out. Ptolemy's friend, the practitioner, enquired how Ptolemy had been so certain about the need for an operation. Ptolemy replied that as a student at Tuskegee he had seen so many of such cases that he had become quite familiar with the complaint.

Also at Bookers Estate there was a campaign against bruceliosis, which was then almost unknown in British Guiana. In the dairy, there were signs that the animals were not doing as well as far as calfing and abortion were concerned. It became necessary to carry out laboratory tests, which the Ministry of Agriculture did, and, to everyone's surprise, bruceliosis was identified. This was quite an issue because the rule was that to succeed with dairy herds all those that showed a positive reaction to the bruceliosis test must be destroyed. The infection had spread to some of the best cows in the herd, and the authorities were unwilling to take them to slaughter. Many people were prepared to purchase the cows, but Ptolemy insisted that the cows had to be got rid of through slaughter and not by disposing of them to dairy men in the community. It was quite a difficult decision to dispose of the animals, but the directors agreed that they must rid the herd of bruceliosis, and so they went ahead disposing of them. Some farmers were trying to make secret arrangements to buy the animals even at the slaughter house, but there was close supervision of the process and all the animals that showed signs of bruceliosis were destroyed. The benefits and usefulness of the campaign became obvious after a couple of years when there was a higher percentage of calfing and of calves, less abortion and better milk production.

Ptolemy had another experience that was a little disconcerting. A well-known gentleman in the community had brought a dog to Ptolemy for castration. Ptolemy put the dog under anesthesia, but before long the dog was dead. It was a strange and embarrassing situation that such a strong dog had died so easily. So, with the owner's agreement, Ptolemy carried out a post mortem to find out that the dog had been suffering from a hernia in the diaphragm and any treatment of the kind done, the castration, would have ended in its death.

Over the years, his ranch work with Bookers was an intriguing experience for Ptolemy. Bookers owned a large ranch at Kabawa in the Blairmont area, which had some 67,000 head of cattle. Every year, flood waters throughout the ranch diminished the calf crop. Clearly, the company had to do something to save the calves. Ptolemy suggested, and the directors agreed, to execute the program of digging canals and making large dams all over the ranch so that, in the rainy season, when the Abari River overflows, there would be dry places in different parts of the ranch to help save as many calves as possible. The result was so encouraging that it became the pattern to develop the ponds with high dams. In the dry season, since it was always difficult to get water supply, several shallow wells were established in the Kabawa ranch area for the betterment and development of the ranch.

Up to 1964, this was a flourishing ranch, and after Independence (in 1966), it was taken over by the government of Guyana as part of the national vision of Bookers. On the ranch, all kinds of practices were done, some that, at the time, were novel. One practice was to dehorn all the horned bulls so as to prevent them from goring the other cattle there.

Ptolemy particularly enjoyed the various demonstrations of simple skills of veterinary medicine then in general practice in the community, especially in Dartmouth itself. Every time he was on leave, he set up a little training school to do all kinds of things, including castration of animals.

Ptolemy visited schools routinely, urging the students to "produce." Many young people were inspired by the work that was done in those days, and they went on to study veterinary medicine. Of course, many of them attended Tuskegee Institute.

Before Ptolemy returned to British Guiana, the Guiana government had never appointed a graduate trained in the United States as a veterinarian. They would appoint such persons only on a preliminary basis on condition that the veterinarian would proceed to London to do further work and gain the British qualification, Member of the Royal College of Veterinary Surgeons. Ptolemy had returned to Guiana in 1958 having acquired that qualification in London, but he believed that students did enough work at U.S. institutions to warrant the recognition of American schools, and he was determined to have American trained graduates accepted to work as fully qualified in British Guiana. It was to his joy that in time this became a reality, so much so that, by 1988, most of the veterinarians in B.G. had been trained in the U.S.A.

# The Political Arena

Many years before, in the early 1940s, Ptolemy had come to the conclusion that he would not get involved in politics, but as he moved around the country travelling regularly between Uitvlugt on the West Coast Demerara and Skeldon, East Berbice-Corentyne and talked with groups of people about the development of their communities, he began to appreciate some of the difficulties that were common then. Yet still, he had no mind to enter politics himself, especially in the front line of politics.

It happened that one Sunday morning, the late Forbes Burnham, leader of the main opposition party, the People's National Congress (PNC), asked Ptolemy to visit him for a while. Ptolemy naturally thought it was a call to treat an animal at Mr. Burnham's home, which was not far from Ptolemy's residence in Bel Air Park. Burnham told Ptolemy that he had not been called to treat a patient, but that his (Burnham's) activists had visited Essequibo and Pomeroon and they had returned with the message that he, Burnham, must find a young veterinarian who had returned from abroad not so long ago and have him stand as a candidate for the Pomeroon constituency. This then was the reason why Ptolemy had been summoned; to the invitation he responded that he had no real interest of taking on politics but he was willing to talk to people since he had been doing that since he returned to the country. Burnham said he was seeking Ptolemy's agreement to stand as a PNC candidate for Pomeroon. Ptolemy argued that he had recently come back home and all his life he had been working only to pay for further education and he was now settling down to a new job. He added that there was one proviso, however, which was if the people of Essequibo, including Dartmouth, were determined to have him as their representative then he would have to consider the request. To gauge the desires of the people of that region and decide whether to enter the race, he must see a written request signed by a large number of people of that constituency. Ptolemy thought obtaining such a petition would be a difficult task.

Within two weeks, however, he was called back by Mr. Burnham to see a document signed by some of the people he knew so well and, thus, he agreed to consider the proposition and eventually accepted the proposal to stand as a political candidate representing the Essequibo-Pomeroon constituency.

Burnham opined that the Essequibo-Pomeroon was a constituency that his party, the People's National Congress (PNC) could win in the 1961 general elections. Ptolemy remarked that he had been in that constituency when Claude Vibert White was still alive and was its representative, and he was not that certain that things had changed tremendously, suggesting that it was not an easy-to-win constituency. He promised that during his leave from Bookers, he would visit the area to assess the situation there.

Ptolemy dutifully spent his two weeks leave in Essequibo visiting as many places as possible, and he returned a brief report which concluded that that constituency was not one that the PNC could win in 1961 because the numbers were against them. Moreover, there was not enough time to do the necessary work to change the situation by the time of the elections in 1961. In the 1957 general elections, the People's Progressive Party (PPP), from which Burnham had split in 1955 (See Introduction), had won a landslide victory, and the elections revealed how difficult it was for the PNC to win power under the first-past-the-post system. Ptolemy also indicated that the situation had worsened because the United Force, the third force, a conservative party launched in October 1960, would interfere not with support for the People's Progressive Party, the party in power, but with the general support of any other party outside of the PPP.

The PNC officials did not quite agree with Ptolemy's assessment because they too had done a survey by looking at the names on the electoral list and deciding how people would vote. They did not know the people associated with the names, and so their survey was quite wrong.

Ptolemy and his assistants in the PNC experienced a very interesting campaign in the Essequibo-Pomeroon constituency. Even though it was the party's responsibility to support him as the candidate, it was largely the people in the area who bore the burden of the campaign expenses, especially in the Pomeroon area where he was not as well-known as he was on the Essequibo coast. As a matter of fact, a campaign on the coast is always much easier to conduct than one in the riverine district. So, for movement in the river, a candidate had to depend on the people in the community, unless he was wealthy enough to hire boats, and Ptolemy was relatively poor. However, people put their facilities at his disposal as the candidate, and the campaign developed.

Once the party workers arrived in an area, they stayed wherever night reached them; they made provision for sleeping at different locations. One interesting feature was the number of visits that they made in various districts, especially visiting individual grants. Though Ptolemy could not claim any great familiarity with boats, during the campaign getting in and out of the boat became a regular activity. He surprised some people with his ability to walk to the distant parts of the grants (generally extensive property owned by farmers), sometimes without shoes, to meet some persons who, in those days, did not want to hear anything about the People's National Congress. One man was so surprised when Ptolemy and his companions found him far aback, because he was keeping far from any "PNC people"- he was so surprised that he later told his friends that if he was not so close to the PPP, he would have supported the PNC because of the distance that they had covered to find him.

Nonetheless, as the campaign progressed, Ptolemy and his companion activists faced difficulty in getting to some places, such as some of the missions, especially to Kabakaburi and St. Monica. Ptolemy, then still a licensed lay reader in the Anglican church, could not understand how a lay reader was being prevented from visiting Kabakaburi mission. And so, the priest who was embarrassed at his opposition to Ptolemy's visit, after a time left the area as it got nearer to the election date and spent the time in the Rupununi. The PNC representatives were eventually granted permission to visit not only Kabakaburi but St. Monica as well. These were predominantly United Force strongholds in those days, but generally the PPP was dominant in many parts of the constituency.

About two weeks before the elections, the party leader himself, Mr. Burnham, along with the chairman of the party, visited the Pomeroon/Essequibo area. One of the largest political meetings was held at Charity, the last village on the Essequibo coast bordering the Pomeroon River. People came from all parts of the Pomeroon and nearby coast, and it was read as a sign by the PNC hopefuls that their party could win the Pomeroon constituency.

Ptolemy advised the leader before he left that very little publicity should be given to the meeting despite the large turnout. For the people had attended for all kinds of reasons, but some of them had decided that they were not going to change from their position as they had voted in 1957 when the PPP had won that political seat. He told the leader that some of those in opposition, even though they were helping him to get around, had already indicated that they were not going to change their political allegiance because he, Ptolemy, was in the wrong party. Notwithstanding the assistance they were giving him, they would not vote for the PNC. Some said this loudly, some in whispers. Ptolemy expressed the view that if any publicity was given to the meeting, it might be difficult for him to continue obtaining help to get around to conduct his campaign.

Ptolemy's advice was not accepted. Instead, news of the meeting and the belief that the PNC was almost certain to win the Pomeroon constituency were publicized over the air and in the press. It was then that the opposition responded most decisively. The non-PNC people discontinued giving Ptolemy the assistance that they had previously given, and services and even commodities like fuel became difficult to get as opposition supporters controlled most of the gas stations. They owned the best boats, and all of these were withheld. It was a rough two weeks preceding the elections, but PNC supporters rallied and the party workers got through to the end of the campaign. On election day, every little boat was out on the way to polling stations, Those who were going to vote for the PNC were determined to do just that regardless of whose boat they travelled in. Ptolemy believed then that if the United Force was not in the campaign, the PPP would not have won the Pomeroon constituency.

When the election results were published, the PPP had won but that was the only constituency that was lost where the combined votes of the PNC and the United Force were more than the votes gained by the PPP. The candidate who won for the PPP was the late John Caldeira. His son, in 1988, was an activist and member of parliament representing the People's National Congress.

The PNC had captured the support of a lot of important people in the 1961 campaign, and it seemed hopeful that by the next election, there would be some improvement toward victory for the PNC for, Ptolemy believed, the PPP had marred their own campaign for a long time. For it was during the PPP's 1961 victory parade that people all over the country recognized how unfit the PPP was to manage the affairs of the country. Ptolemy witnessed the action in the little village of Dartmouth which, but for the presence and mediation of certain influential people, might have resulted in great upheaval as the victorious PPP supporters threw water on people and cursed and insulted them. It was a scene never to be forgotten and, in other places, worse abuse occurred.

The PNC decided to carry out programs not only for the next elections but to change the electoral system as well, for at that time the PPP seemed unfit to manage the affairs of the country. So, the country endured the turbulent years of 1962 and 1963, when there was rioting and a long general strike (See Introduction), even as many of the candidates for the PNC who had entered the political scene, like Ptolemy, just for the elections resumed their normal business and ceased to function as activists.

Ptolemy, on the other hand, had an arrangement with Bookers to do private practice, and that gave him the freedom to do all kinds of other things. Hence, he had enough time to work on the sugar estates and spend some evenings engaged in political organizing.

After much research and hard work, the opposition PNC decided to work towards a change in the electoral system before the next elections. They spent a great deal of effort on this, and by the 1964 elections, a system of proportional representation was put in place. The results in 1961 had shown that the combined popular vote for the United Force and the People's National Congress was more than the votes gained by the PPP. In fact, the difference in votes between the PPP and PNC, not taking into account the United Force, was minimal. It thus seemed certain that once the electoral system was changed it would be difficult for the PPP to have enough members to form the government.

Ptolemy stayed on with the PNC political organization and by the 1964 election, the leader, Forbes Burnham, without any further consultation- since Ptolemy was not accepting any office in the party- decided to announce at the last meeting before the elections that Ptolemy would be his deputy during the 1964 elections. Nobody disagreed, and so Ptolemy became deputy leader for the People's National Congress in 1964 and held that office until he retired from the government in 1984, but he kept that office even until after the 1985 elections.

Between 1961 and 1964, Ptolemy had become a well-known figure throughout the country since he was a candidate on the PNC list in 1961. In his travels around the country, he had the opportunity to engage in meetings in several places. The PNC organization was strengthened, and they proceeded on a campaign in 1964 to ensure that the PPP did not win the election.

Ptolemy had by then travelled to almost every part of the country sometimes taking charge of meetings that the comrade leader, Forbes Burnham, could not attend. He remembered travelling through the East Coast, during that election campaign, when Mr. Burnham had some pressing matters and keeping some 26 "whistle stop" meetings as they were called. One meeting was at Plaisance where, it was said, they were holding the meeting without permission, but, fortunately, no prosecution took place. Eventually, the People's National Congress, in cooperation with the United Force, formed the 1964 government. The British government had to pass special legislation in their parliament to remove the PPP from office.

At Charity, after the announcement following the count at the poll, the PPP candidate for the Pomeroon/Essequibo constituency did not really understand the workings of the new proportional representation system, and so there was loud cheering and congratulations being given to the PPP candidate because the result of the constituency was about the same as in the 1961 elections, that is a win for the PPP. However, this time it was not just the votes of the district that mattered, or of a constituency, it was the total vote of the entire country.

It seemed that the activists of the PPP were committed to do even a worse demonstration than in 1961. So, an explanation was given at the Charity courthouse that the final result had yet to be revealed. That brought calmness to the situation at Charity, and people were able to return to their homes without further disturbance.

Soon after, the coalition was established between the United Force and the People's National Congress. Forbes Burnham was named the Premier since his party, the PNC, won a greater majority of votes than the United

Force. Ptolemy became one of the three Deputy Premiers, another being Peter D'Aguiar, leader of the UF. Ptolemy also became Minister of Home Affairs.

In those days, the difficulty was how to bring people to live and work together. For in 1962 and 1963, there were serious conflicts resulting in the deaths of nearly 200 people through violence and racial conflicts. Many thought that it would be nearly impossible to bring people to live and work together. However, Forbes Burnham took on meeting-the-people tours and visited difficult communities all over the country and talked sense to people, calming their fears. Before long the nation settled down to better understanding and better behavior and the process of development began.

The government had good support from and relationship with the United States of America, and so it was privileged to get financial support for doing a lot of work. Support came not only from the U.S. but from the western communities as a whole. It was in those years that the government built some of the roads and schools, and people were impressed by the seriousness of the development work that was going on.

Self-help became the practice of the day, and so schools that had no buildings and had been kept sometimes under the bottom of houses during the PPP regime now had proper accommodation. The road to Linden, where bauxite was mined, was also built in this era.

Nonetheless, there was always some conflict, during that time, with the United Force. Peter D'Aguiar, the leader of the United Force, was then Minister of Finance. In 1967, an upheaval in the coalition government occurred. At that time, Ptolemy was far away from the capital city of Georgetown, in the Pomeroon, doing some work. For it was customary for government officials to visit the various communities in contrast to what happened years before when political candidates did not return to their districts following elections. Instead the direction from the Comrade Leader, Mr. Burnham, was that candidates and representatives visit the communities and the districts and, in face-to-face meetings, discuss development programs with the people.

It was on one of those visits to the Pomeroon that Ptolemy got the call to return urgently to Georgetown. It was, at the time, difficult for him to travel to Georgetown from Pomeroon because he had committed himself to several meetings. He indicated that he could not leave immediately; he would have to conclude some meetings that were being held on Saturday night and Sunday morning and by Sunday afternoon, if practical, he would be able to get back to Georgetown.

Mr. Burnham had sent a helicopter to Charity on stand-by, and so Ptolemy arrived in Georgetown on Sunday afternoon to a meeting at Burnham's residence, where they then used to keep cabinet meetings. As he approached the meeting, Ptolemy got the news that he was the Minister of Finance, as Peter D'Aguiar of the United Force had relinquished that position. Ptolemy had already moved from the Ministry of Home Affairs and had recently assumed the position of the Minister of Trade. He had not yet completed a year in that position when he was made Minister of Finance and served in that capacity until 1971.

Dr. Reid was asked why there was a split between the PNC and the UF. He replied:

> I was part of that. The greatest- I think the last straw was when Denbow was appointed as a member of the Public Service. D'Aguiar himself couldn't concentrate on his own business. He saw this thing [government] as interfering with his business. There were long hours . . . full time work day and night. I think that was the main reason. He wasn't his own boss any more. . . . Here was a man all his life on his own, and he was losing money, so it was easy for a little thing to set the ball rolling. I was in the Pomeroon when he gave up. He wanted me to be Minister of Finance so they were sending for me hastily. People were already losing hope in Pomeroon so I didn't leave immediately. D'Aguiar congratulated me for being Minister of Finance. We had a good parting. I wouldn't choose to be Minister of Finance . . . in a poor country . . . logic and budget. We are too poor for that logic. There was no real hard feeling when he left. People won't know that.

One incident after the 1964 elections deserves mention. After the elections, whether they had won or lost, candidates went back to say "thank you" to the communities. Ptolemy went to Hackney for a "thank you" meeting in December 1964, and there was a church service followed by sharing of some refreshments. The women were bemoaning the fact that they could not get any preserved fruits (which was then imported) to make cake, yet there was the well-known Guyana black cake being served. Ptolemy asked the women where they had got the fruit to make the cake, and he learned that they had preserved the fruit themselves. Instead of the traditional imported fruit, they had preserved carambola, a fruit otherwise known as "five finger." The cake tasted no different from cake made with the imported fruit. The people who had preserved the carambola were the people of Akawini Creek, led by an old woman named Comrade English, and she had requested that Ptolemy should pay them a visit before going back to Georgetown.

The English family had always been involved in the politics of Akawini Creek, and Ptolemy always remembered the long journey he once made on one of his visits some 35 miles up the Akawini Creek. On that occasion, several small boats with engines, had gone up the Creek. Party activists were visiting a newly built school. The boat in which Ptolemy was travelling had waited until the last to set out after all the other boats had left. Lo and behold, the engine in that boat would not start. They could do nothing else but drift along the Creek and use paddles. Their progress along the Creek, through what was a considerable distance, was very slow and they realized that, at that pace, they would probably not reach their destination until the following morning. What was worse, people began to feel hungry.

It was Mother English who suspected that something must have gone wrong and so, after some time, Ptolemy and his companions saw a little light in the distance. It turned out to be a boat sent by Mother English who was certain something had gone awry, and she also sent them food. It was the sweetest barbecue chicken Ptolemy had ever eaten. However, mosquitoes made a good meal of their boat's occupants, probably taking advantage of the cramped boat with so many people moving so slowly. Yet, it was an event which Ptolemy thought no one who had experienced it would ever forget.

Akawini was therefore part of Ptolemy's experience as he remembered that it was Akawini's efforts that assured others that, given the opportunity, they could use their local fruits to make preserved fruits suitable for cake making. So, in December 1967, when the government had to restrict importation of fruits, Guyana then blossomed forth as a country that could produce its own preserved fruits.

By the 1968 elections, the PNC was standing on its own as it had already separated, in 1967, from the United Force although the coalition stayed on to the end of the term. In the '68 elections the PNC contested the elections as a single entity and came out with a majority, and so from that time until the elections in 1985, the PNC was able to gain the majority of votes in Guyana.

Dr. Ptolemy Reid remained in the government after the 1968 elections, but that term of service should have ended in 1973. However, when the period was up, because of the oil crisis (OPEC had quadrupled oil prices in 1973-1974) and the downturn in the economy, Dr. Reid thought it would be a bad time to abandon the Guyana government, [Guyana was declared a Cooperative Republic in 1970.] In 1974, Dr. Reid became General Secretary of the PNC after the Declaration of Sophia (December 1974). He said it was not an enviable position in those times. He volunteered for the position, the first job in politics he volunteered for, because he thought he would be leaving politics soon and would only spend a year in the position. Instead he remained as General Secretary for ten years, until 1984.

Asked what he would have done, had he left politics in 1973, Dr. Reid said he would have gone to Somerset and Berks in the Essequibo. Instead he had given the land [which, apparently, he owned] to a group of schools to establish a school farm. "[The land] has coconut cultivation and other fruit trees. I would have done farming . . . to so develop it [the land] so it could have been a teaching centre for the young interested in farming. While I was a veterinary surgeon, I visited schools all around, even in the Corentyne . . . to speak to the children about producing. That was the one word I left in many schools – 'produce'". Dr. Reid believed that man is "different from all living things with the ability to think – not only a creature but a creator himself . . . for those who believe in the Bible, the book of Genesis tells that story."

# REID, THE POLITICIAN

Dr. Reid's main focus as a politician was to make Guyana as self-sufficient as possible and make Guyanese a dignified, self-reliant people. He felt Guyanese could reach such goals by developing their land and making it fertile. It is said that he was the real moving force behind the "feed, clothe and house ourselves by 1976" programme promoted by the Burnham government. He had such a large dream that he threw his full weight behind it.

What the government of Guyana tried to achieve in the first half of the seventies decade was phenomenal. We have only to look at the many initiatives and ventures that were begun, specifically by the Ministry of Agriculture, to appreciate the effort that was made to realize this very large, almost utopian endeavour.

However, it wasn't that Dr. Reid was unaware of the magnitude of the undertaking and the degree of hard work it would entail. In a speech to Community Development officers on July 23, 1966, he mentioned that the officers' main difficulty would be facing community resistance to change, and he said that they would need to engender "a spirit in the communities to face up to the challenges of our changing society." Dr. Reid himself tried always to evoke that spirit of meeting challenges head on.

In another speech delivered also in 1966, but this time to teachers graduating from the Government Teachers College on the occasion of the opening of GTC week, he commended those teachers who had volunteered to teach "in remote areas like the Rupununi and Bartica." He referred to the government's effort "to encourage Guyanese to leave the overpopulated coastlands and settle in the hinterland" as he encouraged the teachers to become "pioneers in the call for young Guyanese 'to go south'." These exaltations demonstrate Dr. Reid's belief that developing the land was crucial to achieving a "changed structure of the economy" wherein Guyana would have "less dependence on sugar, rice and bauxite."

Dr. Reid clearly felt that Guyana needed to embark on its own self-determined course which was one not dictated by the developed world and quite unlike theirs. In an April 5th, 1970 article of the *Sunday Graphic,* he is quoted, while he was Minister of Finance, as calling for "radical surgery" to bring about "a genuine revolution" of the nation's economy. He believed the economy was being hampered in its growth by the vicious policy of international aid. "He told the 13th annual congress of the ruling People's National Congress that there was need to wage a 'resolute war' against poverty and unemployment, a war which would require taking 'bold' measures to change the economic system." He warned that "governments too timid to initiate necessary reforms often lose not only their popularity but their mandate as well."

It was clear that, in his political career, Dr. Reid abhorred and resented what he saw as interference from outside forces. He once said that he told the U.S. ambassador that there would be no peace until there was no meddling in another's affairs. The article last cited notes that in his paper on "The world Today in Economic Terms," which was addressed to the 13th annual congress of the People's National Congress (PNC), Dr. Reid stated that

"[A]id is tied to . . . expected political alignment to the donor country in major matters on the world scene and . . . key officers in the underdeveloped countries are subject ostensibly on training to indoctrination [sic.] in the donor country or sent on free trips so that they would become sympathetic to the way of life and thinking in the donor country".

Thus it was that as Deputy Prime Minister and Minister of Agriculture and National Development (of Guyana), for a good part of his political reign, he doggedly pursued a course to enable Guyana to feed herself.

Early in the seventies decade, the government of Guyana announced its programme to "feed, clothe and house ourselves by 1976." This initiative had a definite economic target- to save foreign exchange by cutting spending on imports. The government, therefore, banned a number of (imported) items from coming into the country.

At the PNC's annual congress in 1972, "Dr. Reid said that although it may not be possible to produce every single item of food now imported, it will be possible to provide enough varied foods 'to enable the nation to be properly fed, to provide enough variety in the diet, and at a price reasonable both to consumer and producer'." (*Daily Chronicle,* April 6, 1972, p.1).

When we consider the different projects embarked upon by the government and promoted by the Ministry of Agriculture in a short span of time, there is no doubt as to the serious intent to achieve this declared national objective to be as self-sufficient as possible.

We are told in the April 6 headline article of the *Daily Chronicle* that "activists of the ruling People's National Congress have begun formulating tactics to be used in achieving the objective of 'feeding, clothing and housing ourselves'." It was estimated that some $31.5 million would be saved by embarking on this programme, $14 million alone coming from "feeding ourselves."

Dr. Reid said that employment opportunities would result with some 10,000 full time jobs being created from feeding the nation. He cautioned that these were "preliminary estimates based on the assumption that the present methods of production will be maintained" (p.1).

To achieve this national objective of providing for the nation's basic needs, an impressive number of projects were started in the 1970s and 1980s. For instance, the 200 square mile Matthews Ridge Agricultural Project, with a population of approximately 3500, was singled out by Prime Minister Burnham as the "pilot of Guyana's thrust into the hinterland which must demonstrate to the rest of the country all that can be done with land." Three years after the manganese company, that was previously operating at Matthews Ridge, had left the area and the government had decided to convert it from mining to agriculture, there were startling results.

In this season previous to April 2, 1972 (when the *Guyana Chronicle* article was published), corn production was 15,000 pounds and sixty acres were being reaped. The complex was expected to be shortly thereafter producing the twelve million pounds per year of corn required for Guyanese consumption. The beef and dairy herd, which then numbered 300 head, was being increased for local consumption and export to Trinidad. Other major products being raised on the complex were soya bean, blackeye, turmeric (dye), tilapia, ground provisions, peanuts, plantains and bananas.

Three hundred acres of citrus had been planted and wheat successfully grown, which was seen as an indication that Guyana might successfully produce wheat flour. Meanwhile, soya bean flour was already being produced commercially. (*Daily Chronicle,* April 2, 1972, p.14).

It is perhaps not surprising that the Burnham government's intense efforts at development did not proceed without opposition, and we have some glimpses of this. For instance, we read that Dr. Cheddi Jagan, opposition People's Progressive Party leader and Honorary President of the sugar workers' union, Guyana Agricultural Workers Union (GAWU), was objecting to activities by the union in the sugar belt being erroneously, in his view, interpreted by the Chronicle newspaper as "electioneering, with PPP flexing its muscles since it believed general elections were at hand." Dr. Jagan claimed that the sugar workers had grievances over wages, working and living conditions, and recognition of GAWU. (*Daily Chronicle,* April 3, 1972, p.5).

Nonetheless, with regard to the feeding initiative, it is interesting to read in the same issue of the newspaper that "the PNC congress is likely to discuss the question of agriculture and the availability of land and the drainage and irrigation plans of the government" and that the Deputy Prime Minister and Agriculture Minister, Dr. Ptolemy Reid was to present papers at the convention.

That opposition to its programme was perceived in government quarters is once more evident in the April 5, 1972 *Daily Chronicle* headline: "Warning at PNC Congress: Unite to Foil Wicked Agents", which was followed by the news that included mention that Dr. Reid will deliver a paper on "Feeding Ourselves."

However, the government's drive to inspire self-help and production was bearing fruit in some areas as we read of one farmer/cane cutter's effort in the area of cake, pastry and wine making. His products were displayed as part of an exhibition sponsored by the Brighton (Corentyne) National Youth Club. (*Daily Chronicle,* April 5, 1972, p.3). Further, Marlborough Roman Catholic School in the Pomeroon had cleared virgin lands, and the students had planted hundreds of plantain and banana shoots and St. Lucia coconut palms. This school had sold 800 pounds of the produce it reaped from the school farm to the Guyana Marketing Corporation. Moreover, the school had plans to establish a citrus nursery to sell budded orange plants to Pomeroon farmers.

According to the headmaster, Mr. Flavio Camacho, "Within the next three months, we should have about 5,000 budded orange plants in our projected nursery. With the establishment of the canning factory at Charity, there will be a great demand for citrus plants, and we shall market our own, preferably to Marlborough farmers." The efforts of the school's students were supported by an active parent-teachers association and the school was getting tangible support from the then catholic bishop, Bishop Lester Guilly. Such was the enthusiasm in sectors of the country for the push to develop.

The idea of self-help was an important mantra of the Guyana government at this time as is reflected in at least one of the headlines in the *Daily Chronicle* newspaper: "Help ourselves and save $31m" (April 6, 1972, p. 1), which is what the Marlborough school referred to above was doing. And the government was prominently backing such efforts. Thus, the Deputy Prime Minister, Dr. Reid, announced that the new agricultural development bank would commence operations in July 1972 and would lend about $40m to the nation's farmers. This he said was "yet another step taken towards fulfilling the objective of feeding, clothing and housing ourselves by 1976." Dr. Reid stated that through the operations of the bank, "agriculture production will increase and farmers' income will increase as much needed credit begins to flow into crops, livestock and, indeed, all facets of the agricultural life of the country. By and large," he continued, "the main benefits will accrue to the small farmers who in the past could not get agricultural loans easily from commercial banks." So, the government was throwing its full weight behind those it deemed willing and in the position to move the revolution along.

Another area of government enterprise was that of fish farming as the Guyana Marketing Corporation (GMC) tried to "push the production of fish on cooperative and community levels." They endeavoured to establish "a number of fish farms in several major areas of the country" and to grant "assistance to individuals and other small bodies who run fish ponds in Georgetown and its suburbs." The Onverwagt Fish Farm at Onverwagt on the West Coast of Berbice had been set up several years earlier as an experimental station and, was at that point in time, 1972, being used to supply new farms and ponds with fish. The farm was capable of producing an average of 210,000 pounds of fish annually, which the Fisheries Division of the GMC proposed to salt or freeze for transport to remote interior settlements. In addition, about 15 ponds were to be dug at Matthews Ridge as part of the massive agricultural complex into which that area was being converted. (*Daily Chronicle,* April 6, 1972, p.3).

Meanwhile, the Fisheries Division was continuing with its programme of offering information and advice to anyone interested in starting a fish pond. It also offered, free of charge, a skeleton stock of young fish with which to begin one's crop. Tilapia, mullets and hassars were the fish cultivated by the division. (ibid.)

Further, the Ministry of Agriculture was "to embark on a project to fulfill the needs of the local honey market." It was estimated that if the country could produce the more than 18,000 pounds imported annually, it would save the government $13,000.00 per year. (*Daily Chronicle,* April 7, 1972, p.3).

Dr. Reid was clearly committed to the idea of helping oneself as he "challenged" settlers of the Soesdyke/Linden Highway "to put their heads together and solve their problems" in the process of developing new communities. He suggested that while the old system in the country was built on the dependency and exploitation of the landlord/tenant relationship, the new system introduced by the government involved the distribution of land to the small man and the production of the things we need. He warned that "Unless you are fully involved in what we are doing, you will not be able to change your standard of living." (*Sunday Chronicle,* Jan. 6, 1974, p.24).

Dr. Reid, who was also Minister of Agriculture and National Development, explained that the old capitalist system had left Guyana with too much forest on agricultural lands and had not built roads or the other things necessary for speedy development. He said that "we are now trying to change that old capitalist system to a socialist economy." He noted that nearly 11 million would be spent in capital works in the area that year. (ibid.)

Among the challenges Guyana faced in the seventies were floods inundating the rice field, the sugar workers dispute over pay, and the oil crisis. The oil shortage and skyrocketing prices resulted in an economic crisis. Moreover, although we read in the Chronicle of January 11, 1974, p.9, a report from London that sugar prices had soared to a record high, the following day's paper carried an article that stated that in the previous year, 1973, "severe drought followed by uniquely heavy rainfall during the second half of the year [had resulted] in reduced yields, and consequently the country's lowest output in ten years." (*Daily Chronicle,* Jan. 12, 1974, p.1). Also, at that time, Mr. Erkskine Ward, Director of the Barbados Sugar Producers Association is quoted as saying that "Caribbean countries [had] applied to Britain for an increase in sugar prices to offset rising production costs resulting from inflation." (*Daily Chronicle,* Jan 12, 1974, p.16).

Dr. Reid's responsibilities were wide and far-reaching. Just previewing his activities, in the early to mid-1970s, gives us an idea how far-reaching was his involvement in the affairs of the nation. On or around the night of January 7th, 1974, he presided over a meeting held at the Ministry of Agriculture and National Development that "reviewed the progress of Regionalism since it was established with the six regional ministers. . . . Each region's programme for the new year [was discussed] in depth." (*Daily Chronicle,* Jan. 9, 1974 p.3).

We also see Dr. Reid presenting a bill in parliament aimed at preventing "the indiscriminate slaughter of young and pregnant cattle." The bill stated that the practice [had] posed a grave threat to the cattle industry and once it was passed into law, "written permission [would be required] from a veterinary officer before the slaughter of young cattle, or cattle of the female sex." (*Sunday Chronicle,* Jan. 13, 1974 p.3).

Further, Dr. Reid, in early February 1974, was declaring open a one-week international seminar on the manatee at the Pegasus Hotel in Georgetown. At that seminar, he urged that the international research centre on the animal that was being discussed "be located in Guyana and [he] pledged the full cooperation of the government towards the project" (*Sunday Chronicle,* Feb. 10, 1974). On February 11, 1974, Dr. Reid was slated to "present two bills in parliament, one seeking to amend the Housing of Labour Workers on Sugar Estates Act and the other . . . to amend the Rice Farmers (Security and Tenure) Act." (*Daily Chronicle,* Feb. 11, 1974, p.8).

Meanwhile, projects for which his Ministry was responsible were springing up and being embarked upon at a lightening rate. A "$5m Rice

Research Station was to start operations at M.A.R.O.S. in February 1974, and a new local variety of rice was to be introduced. (*Daily Chronicle,* Jan 9, 1974, p.3). Also, a cooperative supermarket was to be opened on the East Coast Demerara. (*Daily Chronicle,* Jan 11, 1974, p.3).

The government planned to establish a corned beef factory in the Essequibo to produce luncheon meat and sausages. This was just one of "a number of projects [that was being] undertaken by the Special Projects Unit of the Ministry of Agriculture and National Development." The plant was expected to use all the trimmings from the ham and bacon plant to produce a wide range of processed pork products (*Daily Chronicle,* Feb. 9, 1974, p.9).

We read also that "a new type of locally produced Tomato Ketchup [was being] manufactured by the Special Projects Unit of the Ministry of National Development at the Black Bush Polder Berbice Region. The Plant [was to] utilize all the tomatoes cultivated in the area, initially for ketchup and at some future date [would] also produce tomato juice, canned whole tomatoes and soup" (ibid.).

We referred earlier to a citrus cannery planned for the Pomeroon area, at Charity specifically. But that was to be just one of two citrus canneries on the books. The other was slated to be set up at Mabaruma in the North West Region. They were projects of the Food and Nutrition Division of the Ministry of Agriculture and National Development. "The plants were [initially] geared only for processing orange juice from oranges of a specific size" and with the equipment in hand, the output would be "in the range of 3,000 cans per eight-hour day." (*Daily Chronicle,* Feb. 11, 1974).

It was proposed that by the end of 1974, "processing of grapefruit juice and fruit segment in syrup [would] be produced at a daily output of 16,000 cans . . . based on 1972 imports, the installations planned . . . would satisfy [Guyanese] needs for orange juice after four months operation, hence the remainder of the year's operation could be mainly for the export trade. Part of the orange pulp [would] be converted to marmalade and the remainder could be used for animal feed" (ibid.). Thus were the ambitious schemes of the then Guyana government as exercised through the Ministry of Agriculture and National Development under the leadership of Dr. Reid, who was Minister of Agriculture and National Development from 1972 up to at least 1974.

With all these ambitious initiatives on board, it is not surprising to read that Dr. Reid had called on a group of workers to "stop the skylarking." The article notes that while the Deputy Prime Minister's words were directed to "those government employees who 'skylark' on the job so that they can get overtime work, Dr. Reid's remarks, however could well be applicable to the great majority of the country's work force." (*Sunday Chronicle,* Jan, 13, 1974, p.4).

Obviously with all the efforts to feed, clothe and house the nation, workers would be needed to see them through. The Burnham government posited that its program to be self-sufficient was "aimed, not merely at increasing the economic output in the country, but also providing employment for all." (*The Black Scholar,* Feb. 1973, p.31).

It is possible that recognizing the amount of work that needed to be done to achieve its vision of a nation that would feed, clothe and house itself, the government of Guyana under Prime Minister L.F.S. Burnham came up with the idea of a National Service programme that would furnish workers and get the many jobs done.

> According to the State Paper on National Service, which was introduced in the National Assembly on 20th December 1973 'the Guyana National Service is the principal instrument to ensure the emergence and development of the type of Guyanese men, women and youths essential to the prosperity and furtherance and indeed the survival of the Nation, and without whom there seems little, if any hope of transforming our country and our Nation into a great people: patriotic, self-disciplined, self-reliant, productive of goods and services and enjoying everywhere in the country a high standard of living' (Heywood, p. iii).

In 1974, the year following the introduction of the state paper to the National Assembly, the newspapers were filled with articles discussing the institution and benefits of National Service. It was a highly controversial programme that went on to require compulsory service from students of higher institutions of learning, such as the University of Guyana.

"Born in controversy in 1974, the Guyana National Service was dismantled," according to one report, "in 2000," but in another, in 1992. (stabroeknews.com/2008/Guyana-review/12/10the-guyana-national-service; stabroeknews.com/2008/Guyana-review/09/03/society-3)

At the height of its functioning, the National Service seems to have enjoyed some success. One University of Guyana student/participant of the two-month (National Service) Student Pioneer stint, which took place at Kimbia in 1985, writing in 2004, decried the loss of what had been accomplished through the activities undergone in the Guyana National Service. She says,

> the benefits of National Service outweigh the negatives; . . . it is such a great shame . . . to see Mother Nature reclaiming ground on which stood acres of tilled soil teeming with cultivated vegetation – cotton, nuts, blackeye, fruit trees – to name a few. [She thinks it is time to recognize these benefits] because many youths are jobless and idle, and (sic) could only benefit from such involvement; because we have thrown out the baby with the bath water. [She dares to hope that] many others will be given the opportunity of experiencing a revitalized, newly injected, well administered National Service. (Heywood, p. v)

For various reasons, not excluding the economic crisis of the 1970s ostensibly set off by the oil crisis, the government of Guyana did not achieve its objective to feed, clothe and house the nation. Nonetheless, it must be acknowledged that the government did achieve some notable success in getting Guyanese to use local products much more extensively and to venture into manufacturing local food items in particular. However, foreign exchange was very scarce for one thing, and that must have had negative repercussions on some of the government's and the Ministry of Agriculture and National Development's ambitious projections.

Despite all the challenges it faced, the Guyana government continued its push toward developing independently, and the efforts in the area of Agriculture and National Development continued. Some of the *Guyana*

*Chronicle* headlines in the first half of 1979 reflect the state of affairs at that time:

"Oil Crisis: Guyanese must conserve change habits" (March 4, 1979).

A celebratory front-page headline announced that "Big international food drive . . . and jobs for many Abary Project off to flying start . . ." This was a project with which Dr. Reid had very close ties. The article reads

"Over the past few months machines and hundreds of feet and hands and tools have been licking the heartlands of the Abary into the shape of the agricultural world to come.

This is being done by means of an intricate network of canals, drains, sluices, bridges, weirs, revetments and conservancies as part of the first phase of the comprehensive Mahaicony-Mahaica-Abary Development Project . . ." (*Guyana Chronicle,* March 20, 1979).

Also, the last quoted issue carried the following headlines which further shed light on the innovations and challenges facing the society:

"Kaituma cassava factory working overtime" (1)

"Lusignan school expands itself – by self-help" (2)

"Nursery schools start thrift societies" (3)

"Guyana has enough land to achieve legumes target" (8)

"Luckhoo team says in GEC [General Electric Company] probe report Power Board urgently needed to solve electricity crisis" (9)

Further in the March 23, 1979 issue, we are told that there were "Local money deals to save foreign exchange" (1) and "Region 3 increases economic activity" (11), plus "Guyana and Canada sign $6.2m loan agreement."

"Outlets blamed for not getting fish to consumers" (April 26, 1979, 1) and also "Move to increase milk production in East Berbice" (7).

"3/4 million allocated to improve Essequibo roads (April 27, 1979, 7)

"City use clay bricks to build pavements and roads" and "Police continue to fight against crime" both on the front page of *Sunday Chronicle,* April 29, 1979. Also, in that issue, "Rubbish dumping hampers clean-up campaign" (3) and "Cheap fish plentiful" – but more co-op market centers must be set up (21).

Meanwhile, Dr. Reid continued his participation in government affairs on many levels. It was he, who in 1979, performing the duties of prime minister, sent a cable to the St. Vincent Premier Milton Cato saying that "the Government and people of Guyana have learnt with deep sadness of volcanic eruptions at Mount Soufriere" and promising that "the government of Guyana is considering specific ways and means of assisting in the crisis" (*Sunday Chronicle*, April 15, 1979, 1) And we read that, two weeks later, "Guyana sends rice, sugar to St. Vincent" (*Guyana Chronicle*, April 27, 1979, 1).

In a message to the seminar on the Movement of Non-Aligned Countries and the World Peace Council in Jamaica in March 1979, then Deputy Prime Minister Reid endorsed the tenets of the non-aligned movement and pledged Guyana and the People's National Congress' "continued association and active participation in the World Peace Council." He said these movements together with the Jamaica Peace Forces shared "a common and overriding objective – the creation of a world peace and justice" which, he said, were "two sides of the same coin." He noted that the Non-Aligned Movement's concept of peace was "the removal of the structural inequities and injustices which impede the full growth of the human being" and that it has consistently struggled against the denial of self-determination and the maintenance of the existing inequitable economic order" (*Guyana Chronicle*, March 17, 1979).

Then again on May 01, 1980, Dr. Reid was scheduled to deliver the feature address at the May Day rally and parade in New Amsterdam, Berbice, in which "hundreds of workers, including religious and social workers, soldiers, and school children [were] expected" to participate (*Guyana Chronicle*, May 01, 1980, p.13).

In the June 17, 1980 issue of the *Guyana Chronicle*, we read that Deputy Prime Minister, Dr. P. A. Reid was honoured the preceding Sunday at a special ceremony at the Windsor Forest Hindu Temple. The occasion was a thanksgiving ceremony celebrating the awarding of Guyana's highest award, the Order of Excellence on Dr. Reid. "Pandit Doodnauth Tiwari, a priest of the . . . temple, described Dr. Reid as 'a giant of a man who has given voluntary service to humanity' and who was 'always kind and approachable.'" Pandit Sharma, on behalf of the Pandit's Council added that Dr. Reid was always loyal, dedicated and committed to the development of the young nation of Guyana.

Replying, Dr. Reid said that the People's National Congress Party and the government respected all religions. He said, "Due to the lack of faith we lose out in life and living. There is so much to be done that we have no time for idleness, bitterness and confrontation . . . We must love one another," he added.

He was presented with a copy of the Hindu religious book, the Bhagwat Geeta.

In October 1980, when Forbes Burnham became executive president of Guyana, Dr. Reid was appointed Prime Minister in Burnham's place.

In the front-page article of the *Sunday Chronicle* of July 04, 1982, Prime Minister Reid is quoted as urging Guyanese to cultivate good habits of eating what they produce. 'We cannot be independent," he said, "if we depend on others to feed us." This was said "in an address to mark the opening of a food fair at Leonora, West Demerara. "Cooperatives should get into the habit of producing food from local produce," the Prime Minister stressed, and he advocated the setting up of a processing plant in the Region to produce flour, though not wheat flour. (The manufacture of rice flour during this period had some amount of success as Guyanese gradually learned to adjust to its use.)

Dr. Reid further emphasized that if man is to develop and face up to the challenges and difficulties, he must use his imagination and knowledge. He added that "unless we turn our knowledge into wisdom nothing can happen. It is this working together and sharing our knowledge that can help us." [The ideas shared here by Dr. Reid seem to reflect his creation of the Knowledge Sharing Institute (KSI). Through the KSI idea Dr. Reid promoted the sharing of skills and the sharing and distribution of food. Food was made more easily available through the expansion of outlets for local food. Dr. Reid himself, in later years, ate only locally-produced foods]

"In declaring the Leonora exhibition/food fair open, Dr. Reid implored the gathering to accept the challenges of working together so that our people and country can attain self reliance."

Exhibits were put on by residents and by agencies such as the Guyana Pharmaceutical Corporation (GPC), the Textile Unit, the WRSM (Women's Revolutionary Socialist Movement, an arm of the PNC) Textile Design Unit and the Craft Production and Design Centre of the Ministry of Cooperatives. A variety of meals cooked with local produce by several home economics departments of Region Three was on display. The food fair and craft exhibition was part of the celebration of Coop Week 1982 in Region Three.

We read also that "Prime Minister Ptolemy Reid has urged that Guyanese be slaves to useful labour and productive work and to pursuits designed to offer a general uplift in morale." He said this when he was addressing graduates and their relatives at the St. Rose's High School graduation on 7th July, 1982. He stated that "man was a slave to habit and so it was that the history he created depended on the habits he cultivated." He said that bad habits do not indicate hopelessness for the future but that they could be overcome by love, hope and vitality.

He advised the young graduates to adopt a positive attitude to work so as to be able to get the job done with joy. "Persist for success," he said. "The prizes of life are at the end of each journey. Do not expect reward for idleness." (*Guyana Chronicle,* July 09, 1982, 3).

Other initiatives that represent the ambition and vitality of the Guyana government during this period were undertaken. A front-page article announced that "41 new factories registered in 1981." The Labour Ministry "registered these factories devoted to a variety of areas, including garment manufacturing, sawmilling and food processing, according to the ministry's 1981 annual report (*Sunday Chronicle,* July 11, 1982, 1). Also, in this newspaper issue, we read that the "City Council [was] working to improve drainage systems" (3), and on the back page is a directive from Dr. Reid to "Do now what must be done – Reid" (12).

In this latter article, Dr. Reid is said to have "appeal[ed] to Guyanese to stand up for their country by using available resources." This admonition was made at a one-day staff conference held by Georgetown's mayor and town council. The Prime Minister was addressing about 800 workers of the municipality, and he asked them to be dedicated to their duty. He said that if "we are committed there would be no unemployment in this country because if every retrenched person cultivated another half hectare, that would contribute considerably to the development of Guyana." P.M. Reid also discussed the struggles and achievements of the slaves and indentured servants. Stressing the importance of a healthy environment, he called upon the workers to be aware of their surroundings and to strive for a clean city.

The staff conference was aimed at promoting greater involvement among the workers. Some of the objectives were: to build a united and disciplined workforce; to instill the spirit of cooperation and dedication among workers; and to achieve greater productivity (*Sunday Chronicle,* July 11, 1982, 12).

Further indication of the long reach of Dr. Reid in myriad concerns of the state follows.

The *Guyana Chronicle* reported that "The National Assembly with the support of the People's Progressive Party and the United Force (on the night of July 08, 1982) voted on a motion reaffirming the validity of the existing boundary between Guyana and Venezuela . . . All 52 members supported the motion by Prime Minister Cde. Ptolemy Reid who declared that the Venezuelans' position which was challenging the international Arbitral Award of 1899 was wholly untenable and null and void." . . . Having given a history of the border issue, Cde. Reid "pointed out that for over a half century Venezuela and other members of the international community had accepted the Award as valid . . . Cde. Reid gave the assurance that Guyana would continue the search for 'peace and harmony' in the 'friendliest manner possible' but Guyana was resolute in its determination that its boundary would be preserved." (*Guyana Chronicle,* 1982-07-09, 1).

On a much different note, recommendation for improving the lot of children born out of wedlock and their mothers made by a nine-man committee headed by Justice Desiree Bernard was presented to Prime Minister Cde. Ptolemy Reid (*Guyana Chronicle,* 1982-07-15, 1).

In his speech delivered in April 1984 on the occasion of the opening of the Centenary Anniversary Conference celebrating one hundred years of existence of the Guyana's (formerly British Guiana's) Teachers Association, Dr. Reid spoke of Guyana's inclination toward establishing relations and trade with the South. He decried interference in the internal affairs of nations and stood up for "respect to [sic] the right of another state to inviolability of its frontiers and its territorial integrity . . .". He spoke of cooperating with the world community and maintaining good relationship with Caricom and neighboring countries.

Dr. Reid exhorted the Teachers Association to involve itself in the directions the government had established, such as promoting regionalism, recognizing and taking into account the resources of the country "which are of value to educational practice and development, to promote discipline in students both in the educational context and for the nation." He also suggested that the Association make teachers aware of the value of serving in their native land rather than going abroad and that it inculcated an awareness that life was worth more than natural possessions (*Beyond the Century 1884 – 1984*).

Dr. Reid retired from the position of Prime Minister on August 15, 1984, a year before President Burnham's death on August 6, 1985. But in 1985, he was still Deputy Leader of the PNC and Chairman of the Central Executive Committee of the Party.

On January 25, 1985, the General Council of the People's National Congress (PNC)

unanimously endorsed a proposal from the Party's Central Executive Committee (CEC) that the PNC's leadership should seek to engage in constructive dialogue with the leadership of the People's Progressive Party (PPP). . . . The proposal presented by Deputy Leader of the Party, Cde. P.A. Reid, was greeted with prolonged applause as representatives of the Party from the country's 10 Administrative Regions stood and cheered in support of the historic initiative taken at the CEC meeting of January 10 by Party Leader and President of the Republic, Linden Forbes Sampson Burnham. . . . A major concern of the Central Executive, Cde. Reid explained, was that the Party's initiative would redound to the good of the nation. The Party, he explained, hopes that constructive dialogue with the PPP will lead to various forms of cooperation at several levels; that cooperation between the two parties would further cement the unity of our people, (sic) and help channel their energies into the development process.

Through the further cementing of unity, it is also hoped that, as a nation, we will be able to guard against imperialist intervention, further the process of socialist construction, reduce waste and enhance national development (*Guyana Chronicle,* 1985-01-26, 1).

However, at the October 28, 1985 meeting of the Central Executive Committee of the PNC convened to discuss the document entitled "Some Tentative Proposals for the Formation of a United Democratic Front," then President Hoyte seemed to throw cold water on the unification idea. "Looking at the document before him for the first time, he inquired who authorized its drafting, who was the author and similar searching questions." (Majeed, 77).

It was observed that

> Untypically, Ptolemy Reid seemed content with retirement from active politics after his resignation in 1984, and, moreso, after Burnham's death in 1985. This retirement was interrupted by his participation in the defenestration of Hamilton Green from the party's leadership. . . . After Hoyte unceremoniously dropped Green from the parliamentary list when the PNC suffered defeat in the 1992 general elections, party unity was threatened by factionalism and, ultimately, Reid was to preside over Green's grisly expulsion to save the PNC from schism. (http://www.landofsixpeoples.com/news303/ns309073.htm)

It seems that Dr. Reid was named Special Adviser to the President, during President Hoyte's term as Guyana's President from 1985 to 1992.

# Retirement – 8ᵗʰ of May Celebration

During the period of his retirement, Dr. Reid met with various groups for celebration (in a religious ceremony, such as at Christmas). But the first 8ᵗʰ of May celebration took place in 1978 when Dr. Reid was 60 years old. It was the idea of Marcus Peters, his nephew and a son of Dartmouth, to have a "Village Day". He thought it would be the best birthday gift for Dr. Reid. People from the area were invited to come back and pool their efforts in various activities and in one big project. It was hoped that other villages would act similarly, and, in fact, there would be an Essequibean Day when all people originating from Essequibo would converge to the region and engage in development.

On that first 8ᵗʰ of May celebration, "the village school was renamed Eighth of May," the birthday of Dr. Reid, who did not then want anything named after himself. "It was a beautiful happening. Pledges, patriotic songs, skits, tributes, and lots of food all grown and prepared by the [local] folks made for a fine package." (Ainsworth, Ewalt. 05-05-2012. "May 8: Occupy Main Street." http://waltieainsworth.wordpress.com/2012/05/05/may-8-occupy-main-street/1/3/2014)

Diane Peters, 31 years at the time- 1989, said that the 8ᵗʰ of May celebration was a worthwhile venture because it resulted in development. For instance, the Senior Citizens Home that was built at Somerset and Berks, a little village on the Essequibo Coast between Charity and Anna Regina, was part of that celebration's idea. It was a home for able-bodied, aged persons who could engage in activities such as planting. (Further, it is said that the land on which the Flora Nursery School of Dartmouth was built was donated by Dr. Reid's mother.)

Another outcome of the 8ᵗʰ of May celebration was the Endurance

Race which originated from a thought Dr. Reid had left in the schools and was a part of an idea the Ministry of Education was promoting. Though the schools did not act on it, some years later, Marcus Peters took up the idea. At first, the race was confined to Dartmouth, but later other villages on the Essequibo coast joined in. In a letter recounting the events of the 1990- 8th of May celebration, Dr. Reid writes: "The usual Endurance Race started at Aurora and ended at Dartmouth, a distance of 28 miles. This was won by Inderpaul in three hours thirty minutes." (See Appendix).

The 8th of May celebrations of 1989, which took place in Dartmouth, kicked off with the Sunday service at 11:30 a.m. at St. Barnabas Anglican Church. About 60 people were in attendance at the service led by a female 'minister'/lay reader. After the service, Dr. Reid addressed the gathering. Among other things, he talked about the stones planted in the primary school yard as "silent teachers" to commemorate past celebrities of the community. He also touched on the economic crisis which the country was experiencing and which he said was not punishment for the country's wickedness as some believed. He said that he had come back to Dartmouth probably for selfish reasons because it was for him a revival but also to let those growing up know that it was an obligation. Most of all, however, he had come because "I love this little village of Dartmouth." He urged the people, "Christians," to "speak of togetherness. ...You are hearing of things coming out of government control. They must fall into the hands of people. The reward of Christian work must be manifested right here. Don't wait to go anywhere else."

At about 4:00 p.m. that day, the community came together for a day of sports. The youth played circle tennis and football. Dr. Reid, who was colourfully and gaily attired, said he had not watched circle tennis in years. There was also a rounders competition between youth from Dartmouth and Daniels Town. Dartmouth won 317 to 311. Short films of earlier sports activities and other community endeavours were shown, as the young people watched while gyrating to the latest pop reggae that played in the background.

Notwithstanding these events, many apologized for what they said was an unusual lack of activity and testified to how cram-packed and exciting the programme used to be in previous years. The community was disappointed because there was not the usual graduation ceremony for the

Eighth of May Community School, even though the students, reportedly, had done well at examinations. This state of affairs was due, the people said, to the fact that the headmaster was new to the school and did not share the community spirit. Usually, the graduation went straight into the interfaith service which began about 8:00 p.m. until midnight to bring in the birthday. Sharing of refreshments would then follow.

In 1989, therefore, the sports events were followed by the interfaith service. Dr. Reid again delivered an address. He said that there seemed to be more vigour and enthusiasm than at previous services. He also stated that "even Christ himself had to prepare for trials ahead of him. He fasted. ... If we want to achieve anything good, we have to go through that discipline. Jesus had a maximum of discipline. He asked: 'Lord, what would you have me to do?'" Dr. Reid also spoke of taxes of land for a nursery school and about universal love. He remarked, "I sometimes say I do not believe in speaking. I believe in doing."

The interfaith service went on late into the night or even early morning hours. Great reverence was paid to Dr. Reid, almost as to a demi-god. Months later, in a comment, Dr. Reid seemed to address his response to this kind of hero worship when referring to spiritualism. He said, "People do all kinds of things. I'm not really that, but I go to all kinds of things. I really don't think these things are dangerous. Even systems (in the world) – it depends on who leads. To me a thing becomes bad if it leads you to kill, rob, cheat people, to be mischievous. If your set goal is that, even if that is not your set goal, and it happens, it is not a religion. It must be of human being."

Quite early on the morning of Tuesday, May 9th, 1989, shortly after 7:00 a.m., a group of people, including Dr. Reid, left Charity and arrived at Grant Consolation at La Bonnemere in the Pomeroon River. It is a location about 14 miles from Charity and 35 minutes by the speed boat then in use by the group.

At La Bonnemere, the residents were holding a birthday celebration for Dr. Reid, who was 71 years old on the 8th May, 1989. Mr. and Mrs. Conrad Allen, who reared cattle, pigeons, crops and sold gasoline had lived at La Bonnemere for about 15 years. They had an extended family there, the wife's family. Mrs. Allen was a housewife. Mr. Allen, himself, started as a porknocker at Hackney, where he had had good fortune growing corn, peas and potatoes. (In 1989 though, there were only coconuts being grown at Hackney.)

Also at the birthday celebration was Pastor George Garraway, who was born at Henrietta Cecilia. He was the pastor of Friendship Church and District Presbyter of Essequibo Region – in charge of all Assemblies of God Churches in Region Two and some in Region One. Pastor Garraway had met Dr. Reid formally the previous year when Pastor Garraway had requested a piece of land for the church at Somerset. Dr. Reid had granted the land and the congregation now had the materials to build. Dr. Reid said he wanted to see some structure when he came the following year.

Pastor Garraway said his church band was invited to play at the celebration. "Dr. Reid," he said, "is a wonderful man. He's not only a blessing to Guyana, but a patriot. We are really proud of him. Any time it's his birthday celebration and we get an invitation, we are ready to participate."

Pictures were taken in the benab at La Bonnemere. The entertainment programme began around 10:20 a.m. Dr. Reid and Mr. Marcus Peters sat at the head table where there was a birthday cake. Mrs. Muriel Allen chaired the occasion, and, after a few words from Pastor Garraway, a prayer was said for Dr. Reid. Five school girls then sang a welcoming song, and there was a brief talk by a resident of Hackney Canal, Lynette Garraway, who thanked Dr. Reid for the Hackney Canal "to help in this crisis."

Mrs. Allen said, "The comrades see what the Canal did for them, and they come to thank him [Dr. Reid] for his wonderful brain."

Following a religious song from a member of the band- "Jesus the light in the darkness, in time of trouble" - Mrs. Allen offered an introduction to the address by Dr. Reid.

In his speech, Dr. Reid said it was good to be at La Bonnemere at his annual pilgrimage to Essequibo, which was for him a revival and rehabilitation. He thanked the school children and all present for being there. He said,

> In 1934, when they were to start empoldering Dartmouth, a man came out with an axe and drove them all away. The commissioner got afraid, and the work was left undone. I owe a debt to Pomeroon . . . Many people didn't know me

then [referring to the period around 1960/1961 during the political campaign]; some of the Garraways, and Benns, and Stolls and Sluytmans . . . in a few years many have come to know me. They had to find places for me and those who worker involved (sic) took good care of me with food and clothing as I moved up and down. They were so good to me, so when I come to Pomeroon, it's like coming home. It was a lesson of how to carry on a campaign with almost no money. As I travelled from St. Monica to almost river mouth . . . we had a lot of faith. They always supported us. We could always depend on Pomeroon. To come to this place, you cannot say that nothing has happened in the development process. There was nothing like this (Muriel's Place). It is good to come to a place to hear they did something to be thankful for. This is just the beginning. We have much more to do to take care of the schools, building more stellings and wharves so there is continuous improvement.

He acknowledged the development that had taken place in the area and added that "improvement in structures is not the full story unless there is improvement in people so we can take care of the structures."

Dr. Reid said it was good that he and his companions had come early to La Bonnemere so they could walk the land and hear what it and the plants were saying. "The land spoke loud, loud to us this morning telling us some useful work is going on here beyond any doubt . . . a sports ground [is] being developed." He urged the people to take care of the land, to husband it properly and grow fresh fruits and vegetables so that the jungle and marabuntas don't take over for "Nature doesn't like empty space." He continued: "We are created to replenish the earth, to rehabilitate it, make it fertile, let it multiply." He said that in 1971 when the government was talking about feeding, clothing and housing Guyanese, he brought that message, a message of faith . . . for works, a message of hope . . . That is why we dug the Hackney Canal."

Dr. Reid referred to the Economic Recovery Programme, the E.R.P., that despite the negative interpretation given to the initials, was an encouragement to shake off bad habits. "We have to practise hard to do things well. We must sleep less . . . When Christ wanted to think . . . He went into the wilderness where there was no noise and [he] fasted. Fasting – to give the brain a chance to work. ... E.R.P. is asking us to conduct ourselves in a way to cause production to happen. You can only have hope if you have patience. Not now, now, now."

He encouraged the people to use their talents, even if it is only one talent, and not to depend on prayer alone, "Christianity," he said, "is for action . . . Enough has happened in the Pomeroon that shows you can do things, that children can do things too . . . Anything people can do, you can do . . . You have, in the Pomeroon, enough examples to stimulate you, so we can really be sure the Economic Recovery Programme is a success." Dr. Reid spoke of the example set by Mother English in the Akiwini – the home of carambola. "[Mother English] used to make this [liqueur]. This is now exported. You have to use what you have or else it will be taken away from you. The first place I drank carambola liqueur was in Akiwini, in 1964, at a thanksgiving service. Then, the women said they had no fruits to make a cake. I asked what is it [the fruit in the cake]? They answered: 'Five Finger.' Now what is it? Carambola. Then Mother English called me and showed me the carambola liqueur. It has won international acclaim."

After Dr. Reid's talk, the children, followed by Sister Cheryl Benn, sang a song. In a strong and lovely voice, Sister Benn delivered her rendition: "I would like to tell Dr. Reid 'Jesus is only a prayer away. He is the master."

A presentation of gifts was then made: The Consolation Progressive Enterprise vowed to give $1,000.00 to the 8th of May celebration to be collected by Comrade Peters. Also, a gift of a tray, in the shape of the map of Guyana, and glass rests was presented to Dr. Reid by a student on behalf of Hackney and Lilly Dale schools. Then, Dr. Reid presented a cutlass and grindstone to the pastor and school children for use by the school and community.

Following the giving of gifts, there was an open session where individuals expressed gratitude to Dr. Reid, but they also shared concerns over the hardships they were enduring and expressed their need for government assistance.

Dr. Reid encouraged the people to work together and not to depend on the government, even though they had the best government that Guyana could provide.

The church band then sang a song. Someone reminded the gathering that the seeds Dr. Reid had brought as a gift for them needed to be distributed. However, it was time to cut and share the cake.

..................................................................................

Dr. Reid himself wrote an account of the events that took place during the 8th of May celebration of 1990. See Appendix. In 1991, he did not travel to Essequibo for his birthday celebration. Instead, the time was "quietly spent doing some routine farm work."

# Farmer and Family Man

After he retired from politics in 1984/1985, Dr. Reid settled down to a relatively quiet life doing farming at his Supply residence on the East Bank of Demerara. He and his family moved to the property at Supply on the West Bank of the Demerara River in 1967, but they actually started working on it in 1961, when Dr. Reid bought the property. He bought it when he went into politics because he thought he needed to have another income, and he decided he had to have land if he was to live. He and his family used to visit Supply on weekends before they moved there permanently in 1967. They had also been considering buying a place on the West Coast of the Demerara River, but at the time they purchased, Mrs. Reid was learning to drive, and she wanted a home where she would be able to drive a straight, easy route (into town). Dr. Reid agreed to that, and when Minister of Finance Thomas moved to Supply, he suggested that Dr. Reid do so too. So, they bought that property and, on Sundays, they would visit the place and plant fruit trees.

Doc (Dr. Reid) was a great planter of trees. He planted cherries first to stop the grass from growing, but they proved economical as later, people would come to buy the cherries. They eventually had almost every kind of local fruit tree on the land.

In addition, Dr. Reid raised pigs, chickens and some cows. He Introduced the last because his wife wanted to see cows, even though he observed, "Cows and plants don't mix, but pigs and chickens are okay."

Dr. Reid was in a constant process of rehabilitating his property. In the mid-to-late 1980s, the place flooded two years running. He had to have drains dug to beat the floods. He dug some of the drains himself.

He liked to pick cherries and pop them in his mouth as he walked the land. He called them "living cherries." He also had and liked passion fruit and coconut. He was always planting suckers and cassava. After every flood, there had to be rehabilitation as the flood would kill the suckers in some fields. Dr. Reid spoke proudly and lovingly of his farming efforts. He said, "I so like to see coconuts; even when I'm not supposed to plant fruit, I manage to stick in a few coconuts. This is where I spend time, my waking hours (during his retirement). Someone asked me if I don't get bored (once he was retired). I said I don't have time. I go once a day or half a day in the farm. So much to do. There is no time to be bored here."

He pointed out that in the rehabilitation process, he would replace the dying coconut tree with another in the same spot. His land was 10 rods in width, and his neighbors on both sides of his property had done some cultivation.

"What we need," he said, "is good land preparation and organization – water control. I tried that at Look Out. Water control needs good supervision to make sure facilities work...teach people how to manage the facilities or else they can't last."

He had also planted pineapples, although some were flooded out. He said he didn't like to spray as a means of keeping the grass down. "The man who is spraying must be a skilled worker. I have to be with him all the time."

There was a special section that was Dr. Reid's direct responsibility where he was pruning and digging drains. There, he was forced to do some spraying as well. On another side he had a pasture for, as he said, cows and fruit trees don't do well together and the mistress likes to see cows around. There was also a pasture for ducks and chickens. There was a pen that was his son, Herman's, with layers. He explained that "we have organized pastures so when difficulties in getting feed arise, nature will provide grass."

Ruth Chalmers married Ptolemy Reid in 1955. She was 36 years old then, the daughter of Ptolemy's beloved former headmaster of Dartmouth School. They had a happy marriage, though even when he worked with Bookers, he was away from home quite a lot. He would travel as far as Skeldon and Port Maurant while she took charge of the home and tried to see that all went well.

Ptolemy was a congenial and amenable husband and grandfather who left the running of the home to his wife. At one time, she used to open fairs and would even go to the northwest district of the country, but she always "did her own thing" in the home. For a period, she carried on the Women's Auxiliary in the PNC, and for some years was treasurer of the PNC group in Supply from its inception. However, she had to give that position up because of ill health. She continued to hold annual fairs and did some fundraising activities, although because of her arthritis, she ceased to go around. She looked after the chickens and ducks on the farm.

Ruth had a very good relationship with her husband, whom she considered a tolerant father and a well-loved grandfather. They never quarreled but would rather discuss issues amicably.

His wife said that Dr. Reid was "funny" about his food, which made them laugh. He was quite concerned about his health and read late into the night about things he was engaged in, such as poultry and dieting. Yet he did not believe in medicine. He believed one's diet is important. He ate, in later years, only food produced and grown locally. Indeed Dr. Reid used to preach everywhere that "whoever feeds you controls you." (Ainsworth, "Occupy Main Street"). His flour was always mixed with middling, which is a powder from wheat. Whatever Ruth baked, she had to bake his portion separately. He would ask, "Didn't you do one for me?" For instance, when she visited her daughter-in-law after the birth of her third child and first girl named Christine (after Doc's mother, Flora Christina – Doc suggested Christina should be shortened), she baked a cake for her daughter-in-law and had to bake one for Dr. Reid too.

One night he mixed middling with nut butter and told her to taste it. She thought it tasted good, but she wanted to spit out the husk. However, she kept it in her mouth because she didn't want him to see her spit the husk out. Not very long before that, he had read where someone said not sifting the middling made it good for roughage, so he told her not to sift it anymore. He was indeed "funny" about food.

Every Christmas, the police choir sang at their house. Mrs. Reid looked forward to that. It would not have been Christmas for her without it. They also celebrated the Hindu feasts of Phagwah and put up lights for Diwali. East Indian people would come to the house to cook their traditional dishes. Once Mrs. Reid asked if she couldn't use "cook up," a

Creole dish. They were happy to accommodate that and from that time, they had a mix of cultural foods in the celebration of the feasts.

The Reids, over the course of years, had adopted two girls. The older one, Lizzie, first came to live with them. Herman, the Reids' son, concerned that he had to leave his mother to study abroad, had travelled to the Northwest (of Guyana) to find a companion for her. That was when Lizzie came to the Reids from Matthews Ridge. Some years later, her younger sister came to Georgetown for medical treatment. When Mrs. Reid heard that the girl was in town, she immediately thought it would be a good idea to have her live with them as a companion for Lizzie. She phoned Dr. Reid at work to let him know of the second girl's presence and he said, "Oh!" and seemed to have the same idea. So, the younger sister lived with them from then on until she was eighteen.

Lizzie was very happy with the Reids and called Dr. and Mrs. Reid Daddy and Mommy. When she was small, she would go with Dr. Reid to functions, and she used to cut the ribbon to open buildings. She said of Dr. Reid, "I find him very nice to me, a father to me. No matter he talks to me and quarrels. If I ask for anything, he tries to get it for me. If I want to go anywhere, he says 'yes', but Mommy has the last word. He's interesting; he shows you everything about the farm. He tells you how to act with people."

That Dr. Reid's involvement in politics took a toll on him was not lost on Lizzie. Speaking during the period after his retirement, she said,

> Politics gets you kind of confused, and dealing with matters pertaining to government is very hard. After a time, you feel he's doing too much for his age. I used to feel sorry for him because he goes to bed very late, not 'til next morning. Especially at election times you're afraid…a lot of thinking and writing. His thoughts would be far away. You'd have to remind him about things. In a way, I'm glad [he's out of politics]. It is time he is with his family. He's very happy. He has much more time for his farm, working. Everything he does makes me feel good.

Referring to the period in the late 1980s after his retirement from politics, Lizzie said, "Some mornings, he gets up early for exercise. He teaches us to get up early. 'You must get up early if you want to do business.' He goes down with the boys to bring up things from the farm to be transported to town, wherever. There is a different attitude. You don't see that vexation in him anymore."

However, she said, "He does quarrel if you do something in a way he did not tell you to do it, or if you carry the wrong parcel or make a mistake. He says, 'You should have better sense; you are not small children, you must know right from wrong'. But if he quarrels, he comes back in five minutes as if nothing is wrong."

Even after his retirement from politics, many people would come to Dr. Reid for advice and for help with their problems. Lizzie testified that, "If they come with a problem, he says, 'I'm not in the government anymore.' He directs them to other [government] ministers or advises them."

Tara, Dr. Reid's granddaughter, was two years old when she went to live with her grandparents. She was eight years old and in standard two of Stella Maris School when she was interviewed. She spoke of her love for her grandfather even though he would holler on her if her brother did something bad. She liked Dr. Reid because he read her stories. Sometimes, when she didn't want to read, like bedtime stories, he would read to her.

She ate with him often. She would eat all types of fruit with him and she would eat rice, chicken, beef and pepper pot. He liked greens, pineapple, mango, pear, banana, cherry, orange, grapefruit, pawpaw, sapodilla – she named some of the many fruits they enjoyed together.

Tara said that her grandfather worked hard planting and repairing many things. That morning, he had repaired her drawer because it was broken and all her clothes were falling out. She believed her Granny must have asked him to repair the drawer.

She said, "I talk [with him] about work, schoolwork, spelling, math, grammar," and he would help her. "I tell him I'm getting on alright. Sometimes I show him my book. I talk with him at nighttime and daytime. Sometimes, he does go to the back [back dam; the farm]; he's not all the time in the house. He goes out at nighttime. I go to church with him most of the time. Sometimes, he got to go somewhere else."

Speaking of her brothers, she said,

> Nyal [is] disgusting. He comes Christmas Eve night. The next one is the boss for him (Dr. Reid). He is two. Imitating her grandfather, she says, 'Vincey, please. Vince say sorry. That's better.' Nyal and Vince come up here on Sundays. Sometimes [on] Saturday…most Saturdays, but they hardly go to church here. Daddy brings them up and sometimes he goes back. My mother is in the States. She does phone. I don't know when last she phoned. I'm happy here. The only thing I don't like is the blackouts and water shortage. I never went to the States, but [I went] to Antigua where I nearly drowned.

I'm glad I have a granddad like this because he reads stories, helps me with work, takes me out for drives to church, to Georgetown [to see relatives], to Soesdyke. Sometimes the driver or Daddy Herman carries us to Timehri [the airport] for sports.

I get angry with him [granddad] when he doesn't read for me or doesn't give me fruits. He tells me to go and ask in the kitchen. They won't give [it to] me sometimes, but he would most times…

"This year he gave me a doctor set from he and Granny and a supermarket set [for Christmas gifts]". Regarding the police choir concert, which was about to begin, she said, "We usually get more villagers. This isn't the first one [I've been to]. Usually, we get more people [attending the concert].

At Home – At Supply, E.B.D.

Dr. Reid had his own bike and exercised 10 to 15 minutes a day. He said once of himself: "I am a troublesome man . . . always troublesome. I grew up troublesome."

At Supply, he didn't eat regular meals- just whenever he was hungry.

He ate leaves, fruit, bran or middling. If he had to, he prepared his own meals, which were simple and straightforward and involved little cooking.

On one occasion, while discussing some theft of public funds by Guyanese citizens, Dr. Reid remarked:

> This living . . . by stealing, cheating isn't natural . . . I think a lot has to do with the food we eat. Food affects us not just in giving nutrition and making us grow but how we think. A study was done some years ago of meat-eating countries: Argentina, Australia. It was found that people who eat meat are more aggressive – like lions, etc.
>
> When we were children, people couldn't afford to eat as much meat. To get a leg of chicken was a rare thing, but now people eat a lot of meat. I was a great consumer-eating with gluttony. It wasn't good for me. I saw the change; I had to stop.

While at Supply, Dr. Reid apparently played an active role in community activities. On Sunday, October 15, 1989, he was at the church of St. Matthew's parish with a group of about a dozen people. There were harvest envelopes to be distributed for the following week's harvest. One woman asked who had paid for a drum, and Alexander, Dr. Reid's police guard said, "You paid for it, Doc," to which Dr. Reid self-effacingly replied, "That's an advance." Later, looking at his diary, Doc asked, "Anything else, Alexander, that I forgot?"

Then he said, "Sufficient of you are here now for us to sing, Mrs. Charles . . . or if you have a new song to teach us."

He joined in the singing, sharing his book with Kunle, my (the writer's) nephew.

According to Fitz Alexander, Dr. Reid's bodyguard in 1989, "The last time Doc was really busy (with the government) was in 1985 during the election campaign, [but] he is always present for the three days of General Council [of the PNC]." Doc, he said, is very involved in the church. When the priest was not present, Dr. Reid sometimes carried on matins.

Further, Dr. Reid did a lot of work in the community. He sat and made plans to hold a fair, to raise funds and repair the building [church]. Fitz

Alexander said that he sometimes felt that Dr. Reid was not pleased about certain things. "Yes, I feel sorry because you're trying to push something and people are not assisting." The writer certainly got that feeling of difficulty getting a cooperative response from the community. Dr. Reid himself said, at the church that October morning in 1989: "Farming is a difficult thing to do – to get people to help with the work. Who can you expect to come? That is, I tell them I chose to do what I can do myself. I don't have to depend wholly on anyone."

Fitz Alexander testified to the fact that Dr. Reid was a strict boss with whom you had to be on your p's and q's as he liked to see what had to be done is done properly.

Claudette Wilson, Dr. Reid's secretary in 1989, agreed with that sentiment. She said that as a boss, Dr. Reid was nice but he was very particular, considering everything important and to be done as it ought to be done. She said that since Dr. Reid was then (1989) out of politics, her work was not concerned with government but was party (PNC) work or about personal matters. However, people would come to Dr. Reid for advice. It might be a land problem with neighbors or family problems. People came from as far flung areas as Berbice, the Essequibo and Linden. They were men and women from all walks of life. She thought they probably came to Dr. Reid because they heard him addressed as "special adviser" to the president.

Ms. Wilson said that Dr. Reid told people who wanted an audience with him to come very early in the morning, about 6:30 a.m., because by 7:00 a.m., he leaves if no one is there to see him. He sometimes advised people to see a minister of the government.

The secretary said that whenever she needed time-off, she would get it, so if she had to work on Saturday or Sunday, say for an event, she did so willingly. She said Dr. Reid was "always around;" he was interested in what was going on in the community.

# CONCLUSION

To sum up Dr. Reid's impact as a politician, I turn to the Obituary published in *Stabroek News*.

Sheer endurance seemed to be the most distinguishing characteristic of Dr. Reid's political career. Hence his sudden departure from the centre stage of government on August 15, 1984 while serving as Prime Minister, a year before Burnham's death on August 6,1985, was as unexpected as its consequences were unplanned . . . that departure facilitated . . . Desmond Hoyte's promotion to the Prime Minister's office . . . (and his eventual) accession to the Presidency.

Playing the pivotal role of mediator and kingmaker, Reid, at that time the PNC's Deputy Leader, declined to exercise his right of succession to the leadership position . . . (as President) Hoyte . . . embark[ed] with confidence on a programme of political and economic change which turned out to be a reversal of much that Reid had stood for in the Burnham era.

Ptolemy Alexander Reid's political strength was based largely on his unassailable position as one-time General-Secretary and Deputy Leader. . . . Reid . . . enjoyed the genuine support of the African-Guyanese in his home region – the Pomeroon-Supenaam – more than could be said for many other PNC politicians. Deeper than that, however, was his unquestionable adherence to the party line and *unquestioning loyalty to the party leader, Forbes Burnham* (my emphasis). It was taken as axiomatic that Reid would support any position that Forbes Burnham took, and vice versa. Although five years older than Burnham, Reid seemed serenely satisfied with his status as permanent junior partner.

(http://www.landofsixpeoples.com/news303/ns309073.htm)

And for the conclusion of his personal life, I turn to "Guyana Jottings – 2".

After his retirement in 1984, [Dr. Reid] lived a quiet life and was often referred to as an 'elder statesman.' The Ptolemy Reid Rehabilitation Centre, located at Church and Carmichael, Streets, Cummingslodge, Georgetown was named after Dr. Reid. The center gives therapy and basic education to children with cerebral palsy and those with physical disabilities.

[Following the death of his first wife, Ruth, Dr. Reid travelled to the United States of America and brought back his second wife, his childhood sweetheart, Marjorie Griffith. His marriage to Marjorie came as a surprise to some in Guyana. Apparently, Dr. Reid had, around that time, another romantic attachment in Guyana. Yvonne Harewood-Benn, former Guyana Minister of Public Service and of Information, said she did not know if, in marrying Marjorie, Dr. Reid was keeping a promise he may have made.] Marjorie "died on May 25, 2003, leaving him a widower for a second time.

Towards the end of his life Dr. Reid suffered a stroke and was admitted to the Suddie hospital [on the Essequibo Coast]. He was later returned to his home at Atlantic Gardens where he died on Tuesday, September 2, 2003 aged 85." (silvertorch.com/guyjots-2.html).

# Appendix

"YEAR OF INTENSIFIED EFFORT AND
GREATER SELF-RELIANCE"

Supply
East Bank Demerara

Greetings! This is a report of what took place during my birth anniversary celebrations.

Like last year this year's programme included the Pomeroon area.

The main programme got started on May 02, 1990, with the repainting of Flora Nursery School. On the 4th of May, the rehabilitation of farm lands was done and on the 6th of May, the Day of Sports took place.

On Monday May 7, 1990 visits were made to Flora Nursery School and Eighth of May Primary School. At Flora Nursery School gifts were handed out for the children. The children presented a short and inspiring cultural programme for me. At Eighth of May Primary School the children performed two short but beautiful skits.

Later on the same day 45 Senior Citizens had their treat and listened to a discourse. Before leaving each one of them received a parcel of Textured Vegetable Protein. Later I had the annual discourse with graduands of the 10th Graduation Class. That was followed by the Inter-Faith Service chaired by Cde Hoppie, Education Officer.

On Tuesday May 08, 1990 the church service was conducted by Father Bertie Barker and two visiting members of S.O.M.A. (Sharing of Ministry Abroad). The usual Endurance Race started at Aurora and ended at Dartmouth a distance of 28 miles. This was won by Inderpaul in 3 hours 32 minutes.

I again visited the Eighth of May Primary School and had a discourse with Teachers and students and distributed gifts. On this visit I was presented with a beautiful hat, two large table mats and a shapely swan basket of fruits.

Later there was an Exhibition and Food Fair at Eighth of May Community High School where lots of local craft and locally prepared food were on display.

On May 09, 1990 the entire day was spent in the Pomeroon River. At Cde Muriel Allen, Grant Consolation, there was a cultural presentation. There school children from Hackney Primary School joined with invitees from other grants. A brief visit was made to Aberdeen, there I visited a koker that was recently repaired and discussed a few complaints from the residents. A visit was also made to Cde Joseph Benn at Grant Unity, where a meeting was held. This meeting was chaired by Cde Roberts. It was a pre-neighbourhood Conference mobilization exercise as well.

On May 10, 1990 I visited the backlands of Dartmouth and later in the afternoon had a discussion with farmers. The drainage and irrigation facilities have been rehabilitated as one of the birthday projects. Villagers have already begun to do useful and productive tasks.

Then there was the highlight for the village, the extravaganza cultural presentation. Long before the programme commenced the school was packed and soon there was not even standing accommodation. Cde Shamlall who acted as Headmaster when Cde Osbourne was transferred, welcomed the large gathering including visitors who came by minibus. Cde Marcus Peters chaired this event and the Nursery School presented a welcome song.

The show was fully enjoyed and with dancing, drums and songs and verse speaking the excitement was great and full of interest including local happenings in drama, song and verse speaking.

Prizes were distributed to the participants in the Endurance race and students of the Tie Dye class.

I received my birthday gifts then, a large wooden key fashioned by the Industrial Arts students. Unfortunately the Industrial Arts special building is in a state of disrepair but plans are now afoot to rehabilitate the building.

On Friday May 11, 1990 I visited the Senior Citizen Home at Somerset and Berks and has (sic) a short discourse with the residents. The children from the Somerset Nursery School did a short performance of songs and recitations.

A brief visit was also made at Cde Aziz Bacchus Woodwork Enterprise at Anna Regina. It is a good example of what can happen if we seize opportunities around our very environment.

Later there was a meeting at Anna Regina Community High school with Cde Regional Chairman and Party leaders from Supenaam to Somerset and Berks, and of course the attendance was good. I received a beautiful piece of sculpture.

The celebrations this year were inspiring and rejuvenating as usual.

[The above was written by Dr. Reid himself and
delivered to the writer of this biography.]

# Notes

Chapter 1: The Early Years

Dartmouth- For background see (guyanachronicle.com/2016/10/24/the-charitable-community-of-Dartmouth)

Chapter 7: Study in London

Bookers McConnell

"Booker Group plc. of Bucklersbury House, Cannon Street, London EC4- the United Kingdom's largest food wholesale operator with a history in shipping, engineering and distribution.

Bookers had a long history of exploitation of sugar workers through the indentured labour system during the 19th and 20th centuries. At its peak it controlled 75% of the sugar industry in British Guiana and was so powerful that a common joke was to refer to that country as 'Bookers Guiana'.

1835 The company was founded by George and Richard Booker when they bought the first ship and established the Booker Line" (https://graccsguide.co.uk/Booker_Group)

Chapter 9: Experiences as a Veterinary Surgeon

President's College

"President's College was opened in 1985 [at Golden Grove, East Coast Demerara] as the first boarding school in Guyana and the only secondary school to use a more comprehensive and selective application process. The school was founded by the late President of Guyana, Forbes Burnham, who launched the project in 1983 but died before the school opened.

The school allows students to attend without being residential, thereby functioning as a boarding and a day school." ("President's College No Longer Among the Top Five Secondary Schools." Jul 03, 2010. Kaiteurnewsonline. com/2010/07/03 president%E2%/80%/99s-college-no-longer-among-top-five-secondary-schools). Apparently in the period around 1990, Dr. Reid was Chairman of the Board of President's College.

Chapter 10: The Political Arena

"Comrade" In keeping with the socialist ideology pursued during the Burnham era, 'Comrade' (Cde.) was used as the proper form of address for public officials.

Peter Stanislaus D'Aguiar

"In 1934, following the death of his father, D'Aguiar became the managing director of the family business D'Aguiar Brothers. Meanwhile, D'Aguiar formed a brewery in Barbados, Banks (Barbados) Breweries Ltd., which opened its doors in September 1961." He died March 30, 1989. (https://en.wikipedia.org/wiki/Peter_D%27Aguiar)

Carambola or five finger, a fruit; also known as "star fruit."

Chapter 11: Reid the Politician

Regionalism- Guyana is made up of 10 administrative regions (www.guyanagraphic.com/content/regions-guyana)

Cooperatives/Cooperativism

"In 1970 the Guyanese government embarked on a program of cooperative socialism to develop an economic system of cooperative institutions based on socialist principles."

(Naraine Persaud, "A Study of Cooperativism and Change in Guyanese Society," *International Review of Modern Sociology,* Vol. 16, No.1, (Spring 1986), pp.51-67 https: //www. Jstor.org/stable/41420868)

National Service

"The Guyana National Service had its origin in an attempt to solve the problem of youth unemployment in the mid-1960s." It absorbed the Guyana Youth Corps which was established on 1st January, 1968 based on the idea of Robert F. Landor, a UN consultant. "Born in controversy in 1974, the Guyana National Service was dismantled in controversy in 2000."

(David Granger, "The Guyana National Service," Dec 10, 2008 stabroeknews. com/2008/guyana-review/12/10/the-guyana-national-service/

". . . the GNS was in existence from 1974 to 1992."

(Reflections: "The Guyana National Service: Burnham's Vision – 35 years after," Staff Writer, Sept. 3, 2008 stabroeknews. com/2008/guyana-review/09/03/society-3)

"The *Mahaica-Mahaicony-Abary* [my emphasis] Agricultural Development Authority is a body corporate which was established by Act No. 27 of 1977 dated December 31, 1977. It has been established to promote, execute and maintain infrastructural, economic and social development of the approximately 38,000 member community between the Mahaica Creek and Berbice River. This two-phase MMA Water Control Project Area will embrace a gross area of about 423,000 acres and 287,000 irrigable areas in about fifteen years of development. . . . The Abary River Water Control Project is the Phase 1, Stage 1 project of the MMA Area and is financed by the Inter-American Development Bank and Government of Guyana."

(John S.L. Browman, Project Manager (Agricultural Development) *The Abary River Water Control Project*)

Movement of Non-Aligned Countries

Non-Aligned Movement (NAM) was established in 1961; as of April 2015, it had 120 members and 17 observer states.

"The Non-Aligned Movement was formed during the Cold War, largely on the initiative of the-Yugoslavia President Josip Broz, as an organization of States that did not seek to formerly align themselves with either the United States or the Soviet Union but sought to remain independent or neutral." (www.nti.org/learn/treaties-and-regimes/non-aligned-movement-nam/)

Guyana-Venezuela Border Issue

"Venezuela claimed more than half of the territory of the British colony of Guyana at the time of the Latin American wars of independence, a dispute that was settled by arbitration in1899 after the Venezuelan Crisis of 1895. In 1962 Venezuela declared that it would no longer abide by the arbitration decision, which ceded mineral-rich territory in the Orinoco basin to Guyana. The disputed area is called Guayana Esequiba by Venezuela. A border commission was set up in1966 with representation from Guyana, Venezuela and Great Britain, but failed to reach agreement. Venezuela vetoed Guyana's bid to become a member of the Organization of American States (OAS) in 1967. In 1969 Venezuela backed an abortive uprising in the disputed area.

Under intense diplomatic pressure, Venezuela agreed in 1970 to a 12-year moratorium on the dispute with the Protocol of Port-of-Spain. In1981, Venezuela refused to renew the protocol. However, with changes in the government of both countries relations improved, to the extent that Venezuela sponsored Guyana's 1990 bid for OAS membership."

(https://en.wikipedia.org/wiki/Guyana-Venezuela-relations)

"Venezuela has been claiming title to Guyana's Essequibo region for years. However, there is an increasingly more confrontational stance between the two countries, to the point of raising the possibility of an armed conflict between the two nations. The tension was triggered on May 20, 2013, when the American oil giant ExxonMobil discovered 'recoverable hydrocarbon resources in its Liza-1 well at the Stabroek Block with a commercial value in excess of US$1billion.' The Essequibo basin and delta region amounts to over 150,000 square kilometers of territory – nearly two-thirds of Guyana's land area – claimed by Venezuela." (Dr. Jose de Arimateia de Cruz, "Strategic Insights: Guyana-Venezuela: The Essequibo Region Dispute," Dec. 14 2015, p.2 publications.armywarcollege.edu/pubs/3338.pdf Jun 2, 2017)

Caricom

"The Caribbean Community (CARICOM) is a grouping of twenty countries: fifteen Member States and five Associate Members. . . .Stretching from The Bahamas in the north to Suriname and Guyana in South America, CARICOM comprises states that are considered developing countries, and except for Belize, in Central America and Guyana and Suriname in South America, all Members and Associate Members are island states. . . . CARICOM came into being on 4 July 1973 with the signing of the Treaty of Chaguaramas by Prime Minister Errol Barrow for Barbados, Forbes Burnham for Guyana, Michael Manley for Jamaica and Eric Williams for Trinidad and Tobago. The Treaty was later revised in 2002 to allow for the eventual establishment of a single market and a single economy." ("CARICOM A Community for All." https://caricom.org/about-caricom/who-we-are)

General Council of the PNC

"The General Council (GC) undertakes strategic oversight of the policy development between Congresses. This is chaired by the party chairman . . .

The People's National Congress's Central Executive Committee (CEC) is the governing body of the Party . . . the General Secretary is appointed by the Leader."

(www.guyanapnc.org/InfoCentre/PNCOrganisation/PNC%20structure.
html)

Early in January 1985, the PNC had its first General Council meeting for the year. "The General Council . . . is the second highest forum of the People's National Congress – the Biennial Congress being the highest."

The meeting was called mainly to discuss "the issue of political dialogue and power sharing with the P.P.P., the most significant item on the agenda was the presentation delivered by the indefatigable Deputy Leader and Chairman of the *Central Executive Committee* [my emphasis] of the Party, Dr. Ptolemy Alexander Reid." In the final instant "in calling for greater unity among Guyanese, [Dr. Reid] declared that the People's National Congress should now purse a policy of constructive dialogue with the People's Progressive Party on a structured party-to-party basis so that the process of socialist construction could be intensified." (Majeed, 47-48).

The General Council enthusiastically responded to Dr. Reid's presentation.

On January 25, 1985, Dr. Reid in the capacity of Deputy Leader and Chairman of the [C.E.C.] wrote the Central Committee [of the P.P.P.] formally proposing dialogue at the leadership level between the Parties." Dr. Jagan [leader of the P.P.P.] responded to Dr. Reid that he "wanted to consult with the Party's membership before giving an answer to the PNC."

On August 6, 1985, President Burnham died.

In October 1985, Dr. Reid suggested that the Working Group meet to discuss the document proposing a united front. He suggested that the document be entitled 'Some Tentative Proposals for the Formation of a United Democratic Front,' and minor changes were made to the original document.

On October28, 1985, the C.E.C. of the People's National Congress met to discuss the new document, but President Hoyte did not receive it congenially (Majeed, 47-77).

Hamilton Green

"was regarded as part of the troika – Burnham, Green, Reid – which wielded real power in the PNC" ("Ptolemy Reid: The Last Hard Man," http://www.landofsixpeoples.com/news303/ns309073.htm)

"Guyanese Mayor Georgetown (1994-); Prime Minister of Guyana (6-Aug-1985 to 9-Oct-1992); Guyana Minister First Deputy Prime Minister (1983-85); Guyanese Official Vice President (1980-83): Good and Green Guyana Party (1993-); People's National Congress (Guyana) General Secretary (1962-74) ("Hamilton Green," www.nndb.com/people/573/000202964/)

Chapter 12: Retirement – 8th of May Celebration

A grant – a plot of land like a plantation but on a somewhat smaller scale.

Henrietta Cecilia – a village on the Essequibo Coast in Region 2, Pomeroon-Supenaam

Hackney – "a village in Guyana standing on the east bank of the Pomeroon River, 11km from its mouth. Formerly the business centre for residents of the coconut estates of the Lower Pomeroon River. Hackney is still of some importance. It provides a primary school and church for residents of the surrounding area." (https://en.wikipedia.org/wiki/Hackney_Guyana)

Benab

A benab is a large tent-like structure with a triangular/cone-like roof where gatherings are held in the Amerindian culture.

"Undeniably a brilliant exhibition of environmental engineering, these massive indigenous edifices utilize local woods and tree barks, leaves, branches, straws, vines and palm, and can still remain standing through many generations. Interestingly too, while the benab towers into the skyline, the construction is almost solely handcrafted with limited use of modern tools and equipment." (guyanachronicle.com/2017/09/10/the-benab-a-prized-legacy-of-indigenous-architecture)

Economic Recovery Programme- ERP

"The Hoyte government signaled its commitment to reform in 1988 when it announced a far-reaching Economic Recovery Program(ERP). The plan had four interrelated objectives: to restore economic growth, to incorporate the parallel economy into the official economy, to eliminate external and internal payments imbalances, and to normalize Guyana's financial relations with its foreign creditors. (www. country-data.com/cgi-bin/query/r-5425.html)

Chapter 13: "Farmer and Family Man"

Look Out

"Look Out is a tiny village on the East Bank Essequibo, with no more than 200 residents, skirted by Grove and Naamryck. Most of the villagers are farmers. . . . 'Look Out was a special pilot project that was given in the Burnham government for persons to grow their own food and rear their own meat. The project started out with 24 farmers.'" ((https://www.stabroeknews.com/2017/sunday/04/16/look-out/)

Pepperpot

Pepperpot is a popular Guyanese sauce/dish of Amerindian origin that is made with cassareep (a special sauce from the cassava root), lots of meat, and, traditionally, hot peppers.

"Appendix"

Koker

A koker is a tall wooden structure that sits over a canal and allows for the passage/restriction of water.

"Georgetown is below sea level and bordered by the ocean and a river so it is protected by a seawall and dikes. Spaced along these barriers are "sluices" (canals) and "kokers" (sluice gates). At low tide they can be opened to drain the city." ([www.ibike.org/ibike/guyana/essay/1-Georgetown.htm](www.ibike.org/ibike/guyana/essay/1-Georgetown.htm))

"Sluices and Kokers . . . Both structures are used for water regulation; sluices for irrigation and kokers for drainage." (https://www.stabroeknews. com/2013/opinion/letters/09/02/sluices-and-kokers/)

# REFERENCES

Admin/Ravena Gildharie (Sept. 10, 2017). "The Benab – A Prized Legacy of Indigenous Architecture." guyanachronicle.com/2017/09/10/the-benab-a-prized-legacy-of-indigenous-architecture

Admin (Oct. 24,2016). "The Charitable Community of Dartmouth." guyanachronicle.com/2017/10/24/the-charitable-community-of-Dartmouth

Ainsworth, Ewalt (May 5,2012). "May 8: Occupy Main Street." http://waltieainsworth.wordpress.com/2012/05/05/may-8-occupy-main-street/

"Apan jaat." www.landofsixpeoples.com/news02gyltns203205.htm

Bacchus, M.K. (1980). *Education for Development or Underdevelopment.* Ontario, Canada: Wilfrid Laurier University Press.

Booker Group. https://gracesguide.co.uk/Booker-Group

Browman, John S.L. *The Abary River Water Control Project.* Georgetown: University of Guyana.

"CARICOM A Community for All." https://caricom.org/about-caricom/who-we-are

"A Conversation with Forbes Burnham." Interview by Marvin X. *The Black Scholar.* Feb. 1973, 24-31.

*Countries of the World and Their Leaders Yearbook 2013*, 981-983.

Dhanraj, Joanna. (April 16, 2017). "Look Out." https://www.stabroeknews.com/2017/sunday/04/16/look-out/

"Dr. Reid's Wars of Radical Surgery." *Sunday Graphic*, April 5, 1970.

"General Council of the PNC." www.guyanapnc.org/InfoCentre PNCOrganisation/PNC%20Structure.html

Granger, David (Dec. 10, 2008). "The Guyana National Service." stabroeknews.com/2008/Guyana-review/12/10/the-guyana-national-service/

*Guyana Chronicle/Sunday Chronicle*, 1979/1985.

"Guyana Cultural Tour: Georgetown." www.ibike.org/ibike/guyana/essay/1-Georgetown.htm

"Guyana – The Economic Recovery Program - Country Data." www.country-data.com/cgi-bin/query/r-5425-html

*Guyana Handbook 1974.*

"Guyana Jottings – 2." Silvertorch.com/guyjots-2html

"Guyana – Venezuela Border Issue." https://en.wikipedia.org/wiki/Guyana-Venezuela-relations

*Guyana Yearbook 1964.*

*Guyana Yearbook 1965.*

"Hackney." https://en.wikipedia.org/wiki/Hackney-Guyana

"Hamilton Green." www.nndb.com/people/573/000202964

Heywood, C. Theresa (2004). *I Was There: My Stint in the Guyana National Service*. Guyana National Printers Ltd.

Jackson, Ruel (Sept. 4, 2003). "Ptolemy Reid Passes On." Guyana Chronicle. http://www.landofsixpeoples.com/news303/nc309045.htm

Jagan, Cheddi (1966). *The West on Trial*. Berlin: Seven Seas Publishers 1980.

Lutchman, Harold A. (1974). *From Colonialism to Cooperative Republic: Aspects of Political Development in Guyana*. University of Puerto Rico: Institute of Caribbean Studies.

Majeed, Halim (2005). *Forbes Burnham: National Reconciliation and National Unity 1984- 1985*. Global Communications Publishing, 47-77.

Nascimento, C.A. and R.A. Burrowes (1970). *A Destiny to Mould: Selected Speeches by the Prime Minister of Guyana*. Introduction. New York: Africana Publishing Company.

"Non-Aligned Movement (NAM)." www.nti.org/learn/treaties-and-regimes/non-aligned-movement-nam/

"Obituary Ptolemy Reid: The Last Hard Man." Sept. 7, 2003. http://www.landof sixpeoples.com/news303/ns309073.htm

Persaud, Naraine (Spring, 1986). "A Study of Cooperativism and Change in Guyanese Society." *International Review of Modern Sociology* Vol.16, No.1, 51-67 https.//www.Jstor.org/stable/41420868

"Peter Stanislaus D'Aguiar." https://en.wikipedia.org/wiki/Peter_D%27 Aguiar

"President's College No Longer Among the Top Five Secondary Schools." Jul 03, 2010. Kaiteurnewsonline.com/2010/07/03 president%E2%/80%/99s-college-no-longer-among- top-five-secondary-schools

"Regions of Guyana." www.guyanagraphic.com/content/regions-guyana

Singh, Jai Narine (1996). *Guyana: Democracy Betrayed A Political History 1948-1993* Kinston CSO, Jamaica: Kingston Publishers Ltd.

Staff Writer (Sept. 3, 2008). "Reflections: The Guyana National Service: Burnham's Vision- 35 Years After." stabroeknews.com/2008/guyana-review/09/03/society-3

Staff Writer (Sept. 2, 2013). "Sluices and Kokers." https://www.stabroeknews.com/2013/opinion/letters/09/02/sluices-and-kokers/

"Strategic Insights Guyana-Venezuela: The Essequibo Region Dispute." Dec. 14, 2015. p2 publications.armywarcollege.edu/pubs/3338.pdf June 2, 2017

# About the Author

The author is herself a native of Guyana, who, like Dr. Reid, was born in the Pomeroon-Supernaam region. A retired teacher of English, she lived a major segment of her adult years under the Burnham regime in which Dr. Reid served. She spent hours in dialogue with Dr. Reid in his retirement years and accompanied him at events over which he presided and/or was honored.

At the end of 1990, she moved to the United States of America, where she now resides.

Printed in the United States
By Bookmasters